Campaign • 184

Stalingrad 1942

Peter Antill • Illustrated by Peter Dennis

First published in Great Britain in 2007 by Osprey Publishing,
PO Box 883, Oxford, OX1 9PL, UK
PO Box 3985, New York, NY 10185-3985, USA
Email: info@ospreypublishing.com

Osprey Publishing, part of Bloomsbury Publishing Plc

Transferred to digital print on demand 2015.

First published 2007
6th impression 2013

Printed and bound by PrintOnDemand-Worldwide.com,
Peterborough, UK.

A CIP catalogue record for this book is available from the
British Library.

ISBN: 978 1 84603 028 4

Page layout by Scribe, Oxford, UK
Index by Alison Worthington
Maps by The Map Studio Ltd
3D bird's-eye views by The Black Spot
Originated by United Graphic, Singapore
Typeset in Helvetica Neue and ITC New Baskerville

The Woodland Trust
Osprey Publishing are supporting the Woodland Trust,
the UK's leading woodland conservation charity, by funding
the dedication of trees.

www.ospreypublishing.com

Author's note

What is becoming evident in researching campaigns, even
those that are relatively recent such as those in the Second
World War, is the number of instances where there is
disagreement regarding certain facts in many of the published
books, articles, manuscripts and online sources. Where this
has occurred I have made an informed guess as to which way
to go but if any fact is indeed wrong, then I can only apologise
in advance.

Author's acknowledgements

I would like to thank Nik Cornish and Stavka, as well
as Yvonne Oliver and the staff of the Photographic Department
of the Imperial War Museum for allowing me to use the
photographs reproduced in this publication.

A big thank you goes to Alexander Stilwell, Kate Flintham
and everyone at Osprey for their patience and encouragement
during this, my third book for them.

A final thank you goes to my wife, Michelle, my parents,
David and Carole, and my parents-in-law, Sally and Alan, for
their patience, encouragement and enthusiasm.

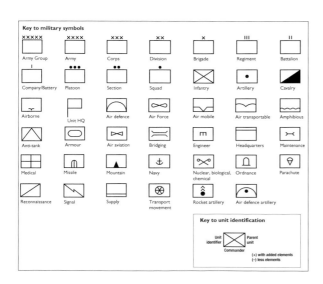

Stalingrad 1942

CONTENTS

THE EASTERN FRONT, MAY 1942

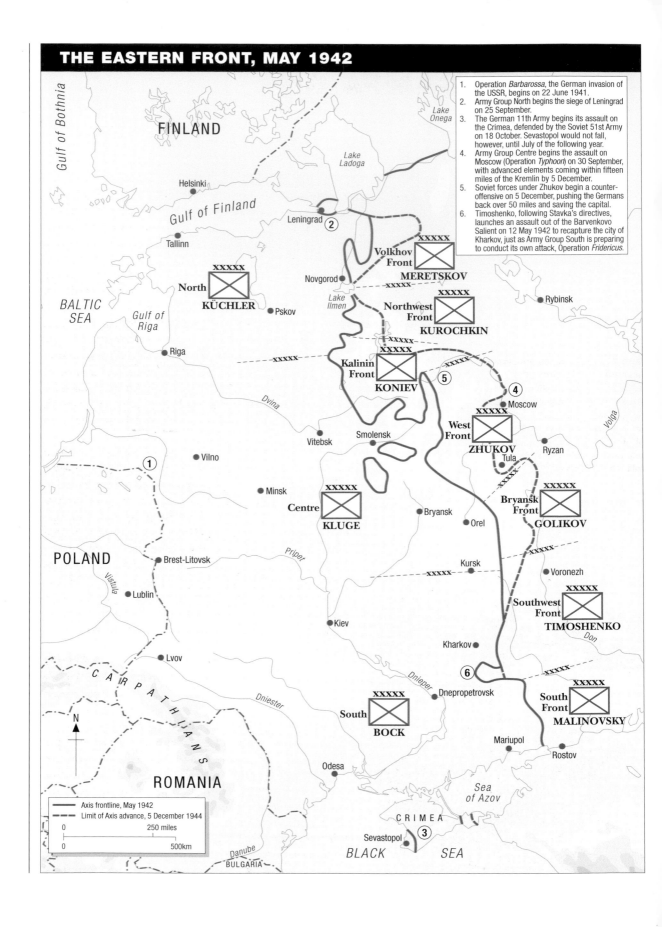

1. Operation *Barbarossa*, the German invasion of the USSR, begins on 22 June 1941.
2. Army Group North begins the siege of Leningrad on 25 September.
3. The German 11th Army begins its assault on the Crimea, defended by the Soviet 51st Army on 18 October. Sevastopol would not fall, however, until July of the following year.
4. Army Group Centre begins the assault on Moscow (Operation *Typhoon*) on 30 September, with advanced elements coming within fifteen miles of the Kremlin by 5 December.
5. Soviet forces under Zhukov begin a counter-offensive on 5 December, pushing the Germans back over 50 miles and saving the capital.
6. Timoshenko, following Stavka's directives, launches an assault out of the Barvenkovo Salient on 12 May 1942 to recapture the city of Kharkov, just as Army Group South is preparing to conduct its own attack, Operation *Fridericus*.

FINLAND

Gulf of Bothnia

Lake Onega

Lake Ladoga

Helsinki

Gulf of Finland

Tallinn

Leningrad ②

Volkhov Front

XXXXX

MERETSKOV

Novgorod

BALTIC SEA

Gulf of Riga

North

XXXXX

KÜCHLER

Pskov

Lake Ilmen

Rybinsk

Northwest Front

XXXXX

KUROCHKIN

Riga

Dvina

Kalinin Front

XXXXX

KONIEV

⑤

④

Moscow

Volga

Vitebsk

Smolensk

West Front

XXXXX

ZHUKOV

Tula

Ryzan

Vilno

Minsk

Centre

XXXXX

KLUGE

Bryansk

Orel

Bryansk Front

XXXXX

GOLIKOV

POLAND

Brest-Litovsk

Pripet

Kursk

Voronezh

Vistula

Lublin

Kiev

Southwest Front

XXXXX

TIMOSHENKO

Don

Lvov

Kharkov

C A R P A T H I A N S

Dniester

Dnieper

⑥

Dnepropetrovsk

South Front

XXXXX

MALINOVSKY

N

South

XXXXX

BOCK

Mariupol

Rostov

ROMANIA

Odesa

Sea of Azov

Axis frontline, May 1942

Limit of Axis advance, 5 December 1944

0   250 miles

0   500km

Danube

BULGARIA

CRIMEA

Sevastopol ③

BLACK   SEA

ORIGINS OF THE CAMPAIGN

The battle for Stalingrad is one of the most decisive turning points in twentieth-century military history. It was here, on the banks of the Volga river that the Wehrmacht was decisively defeated by the Red Army, which only a few months earlier had seemed to be close to collapse. The Red Army fought and defeated (at enormous cost, it must be said), not the under-strength, desperate formations that would try to defend Berlin almost three years later, but one of the largest and best equipped army formations on the Eastern Front at that time – Friedrich Paulus' 6th Army. With the annihilation of the 6th Army, the Germans began to lose the initiative in the east and it was viewed as the single most catastrophic defeat of German arms since Napoleon's destruction of the Prussian Army at Jena–Auerstadt in 1806. After the failure of Operation *Zitadelle* (*Citadel*) in July 1943, the German Army would have to fight a war of survival against an enemy quickly gaining in strength and eager for revenge, culminating in the Soviet attack on Berlin in April 1945.

The origins of the battle lay in the ideological conflict between Nazism and Communism, enshrined in the Nazi idea of *Lebensraum* (living space). This living space would be needed if Nazi Germany was to grow and secure immunity from the Allied blockade. Despite the temporary normal-ization of relations between the two countries before the outbreak of the Second World War, Hitler always intended to attack the USSR in order to destroy Nazism's main ideological opponent, to gain the economic, industrial and agricultural resources of Eastern Europe and also to induce Britain to make peace by demonstrating absolute German control of continental Europe.

On 22 June 1941, the Wehrmacht invaded the Soviet Union in Operation *Barbarossa*, the largest military operation of all time. The Wehrmacht would once again use the blitzkrieg tactics employed so successfully in Poland, Western Europe and the Balkans. *Barbarossa* itself evolved out of a plan first put together by GenMaj Marcks in August 1940. The Red Army would be destroyed in two phases. The first phase would see the elimination of forces near the border in a series of encirclements. The agricultural and economic value of the land in the western Soviet Union was such that the Red Army would be reluctant to trade space for time and would have an incentive to fight for territory. The Soviet forces could not be

German Panzergrenadiers resting near a Panzer IV during the advance towards Stalingrad. The Panzer IV was originally designed as an infantry-support medium tank, to complement the Panzer III, which had been originally intended to fulfil the anti-tank role. (IWM, HU5146)

allowed to withdraw into the interior behind the Dvina and Dnepr rivers – the Germans had to avoid a positional campaign at all costs. In the second phase, the remaining Soviet forces would be destroyed in a decisive battle for Moscow. The loss of the political, communications, cultural and economic centre along with another enormous military defeat would achieve victory in a single campaign (something that German strategy always sought to achieve).

This broad outline formed the basis of Führer Directive No. 21, published on 18 December 1940, which identified the main objectives for the first phase of the operation but not the second. This lack of clear strategic objectives and detailed planning would come back to haunt the Germans during operations in the second phase when argument and improvisation revealed the lack of a coherent plan. The German forces committed to *Barbarossa* numbered over three million men, 3,300 armoured fighting vehicles, 600,000 motor vehicles and 625,000 horses and, along with their Axis allies, were organized into three army groups. Army Group North under GFM Ritter von Leeb would cut off Soviet forces in the Baltic region and strike for Leningrad; Army Group Centre under GFM Fedor von Bock would encircle the Soviet forces between Brest and Minsk then strike for Smolensk; Army Group South under GFM Gerd von Rundstedt would surround the Soviet forces between Kiev and Odessa, and then strike for Kharkov. The Wehrmacht, therefore, would attack the Soviet Union with everything they could muster, but there was little depth – it could not afford to become engaged in a positional and logistically intense campaign. That everything depended upon a short, decisive campaign is underscored by the lack of contingency planning should the campaign have to be fought into the winter months, let alone 1942. This is not to say that German commanders were unaware of the potential supply problems (there were, for example, plans to convert the Russian railway gauge) but the confidence generated by the recent victories meant that a sustained effort to tackle them did not materialize. This meant that *Barbarossa* was an enormous gamble. The gamble almost paid off thanks to the Soviet Premier, Josef Stalin, who refused to allow the Red Army to trade space for time and kept all incoming intelligence about the impending German attack to himself, allowing the Wehrmacht to achieve strategic, operational and tactical surprise and to destroy the Red Army on the border.

The German attack on 22 June began with an enormous Luftwaffe assault on the Red Air Force. It struck over 60 airfields, destroying over 1,200 planes on the ground and those that managed to get airborne were quickly shot down, thus establishing complete air superiority. It then proceeded to make life extremely difficult for Soviet forces to try to resist the German blitzkrieg as it smashed communications, interdicted movement of reserves, interrupted logistics and destroyed command and control. The forces on the border were quickly overrun,

Soviet infantry armed with PPSh-41 sub-machineguns. Zhukov played a dangerous game while the battle for the city raged. He kept feeding just enough troops into the fight to make sure the Germans did not take control completely and keep their attention focused there, while he built up his reserves to launch a counteroffensive. (IWM, RR1210)

thus rendering the concept of forward defence an irrelevance. It would now be a war of manoeuvre which only one side was capable of winning. Army Group Centre's two Panzer groups (2nd and 3rd) completed a double envelopment near Minsk, in conjunction with the 4th and 9th Armies. By 1 July, the Western Front had virtually been destroyed, with over 400,000 Soviet troops captured. A significant number, however, managed to escape eastwards as the 3rd Panzer Group had had to temporarily relinquish the 12th Panzer Division to help the 9th Army at Bialystok. The armoured groups then crossed the Dnepr and Dvina rivers and headed for Smolensk with the intention of creating another enormous encirclement. Halder believed this would encourage Hitler to nominate Moscow as the main campaign objective for the second phase. For the time being, however, Hitler failed to do so, especially as Army Group North had managed to smash its way through the Northwest Front and advance towards Leningrad. The difficult terrain had prevented the Germans from encircling the Soviet 8th and 11th Armies but Panzer Group 4 had managed to advance through the Baltics so quickly that a short pause was ordered so that the 16th and 18th Armies could catch up. Army Group South, however, found the going much more difficult, especially after the element of surprise had worn off. Stavka (the Soviet High Command) had thought that the main German effort would be in the south and so the Southwest Front contained some of the best units within the Red Army. The 1st Panzer Group finally managed to break through and turned south, moving in the direction of Kiev. In conjunction with the 11th and 17th Armies, and Stalin's order that they should not give up the Ukraine, the Germans netted over 100,000 prisoners and tore an enormous hole in the Southwest Front's defences. Army Group South's position improved but the vulnerability of its northern flank worried Hitler, something that would prove to have a decisive impact on the campaign.

By the 1 August 1941, the Soviet position was hopeless with over two million troops killed or captured and German forces only some 250 miles from Moscow after reducing the Smolensk pocket. Halder, along with the majority of the German General Staff, believed that, after a short respite for replenishment and consolidation, the main effort should be directed at Moscow, whose importance, he believed, would force the Red Army to defend it regardless of what was happening elsewhere and this would present an opportunity for the Germans to achieve an enormous encirclement and thus a strategic victory. On 19 July, however, Hitler had issued Führer Directive No. 33, which diverted 3rd Panzer Group to help Army Group North in its drive for Leningrad and 2nd Panzer Group to help Army Group South, leaving only the infantry forces of Army Group Centre to continue to push on towards Moscow. This undermined the very speed and tempo that had so far avoided a positional war, with Hitler in effect having rejected Halder's idea of making Moscow the catalyst of a major encirclement. This caused a huge row within the German High Command (OKW) just at the time when the Soviets were in complete disarray. The argument arose because there had been no detailed planning as to the objectives for the campaign and, despite the obvious German tactical superiority, they could not sustain the grand sweeping envelopments across the entire front. German resources had to be carefully husbanded for each decisive battle. Hitler wavered between the destruction of the Red Army and securing Leningrad and the Ukraine. The latter would be necessary for a long war, but the former would enable the Wehrmacht to win the war in a single campaign thus allowing the Germans to secure the territory in the east at their leisure. The main issue was time: if the Germans had paused to consolidate their strength and launched an operation aimed at Moscow in late August 1941, it is extremely unlikely that the Red Army would have been able to stop the Wehrmacht. This single issue, one that should have been settled before Operation *Barbarossa* was even launched, played a key role in saving the Soviet Union from defeat in 1941.

Hitler's orders were carried out and 2nd Panzer Group moved south on 21 August to link up with 1st Panzer Group moving north, at Lokhvitsa, east of Kiev, on 16 September. They formed the outer encirclement, while 17th and 2nd Armies completed the inner encirclement. Stalin, who had been warned to evacuate Kiev by Stavka, refused to allow an immediate breakout with the result that, after some intense fighting, around 650,000 Soviet soldiers surrendered. Hitler then issued Directive No. 35 on 6 September that ordered the rapid reinforcement of Army Group Centre with the aim of destroying the Soviet forces east of Smolensk as a prelude to an advance on Moscow. The offensive by Army Group Centre against Moscow, Operation *Typhoon*, started on 30 September 1941, nine weeks after the fall of Smolensk. The vast distances across the western Soviet Union and time now began to take their toll as the Germans raced to beat the ultimate deadline – the onset of the Russian winter. By 2 October, Army Group Centre, reinforced by 4th Panzer Group and having its own 2nd and 3rd Panzer Groups, broke through the Soviet defences. At Vyazma they encircled the Soviet Western and Reserve Fronts, while the Bryansk Front was destroyed by the 2nd Panzer Group and 2nd Army, some 150 miles to the south. The Red Army lost over 600,000 troops in these encirclements and, with their defences shattered, it seemed as if the Germans would be able to take Moscow at will. A few days later, however, the autumn rains began and the German advance almost ground to a halt as the dirt roads and dust tracks turned into quagmires. If the Germans had started their offensive towards Moscow in late August or early September, they would have still broken through the Soviet lines as they did in October, but would have been able to capitalize upon it almost immediately, given the better weather. One of the greatest military manoeuvres of all time, the Kiev encirclement, actually badly damaged the Germans' chances of defeating the Soviet Union in a single campaign.

By this point, the German forces approaching Moscow were tired and the Panzers were battling increasing wear and tear. Although they did not possess the depth and reserves to fight a positional battle of attrition, they would have to in order to achieve victory. General Zhukov, appointed to command the Western Front on 10 October, had several factors to his advantage. First, the terrain around Moscow was made of many small forests, areas of marshland and rivers that would help to channel the Germans into identifiable axes of advance and, especially in winter, prevent them from conducting the sweeping manoeuvres that had previously brought them success. Second, it was obvious what the Germans would be trying to accomplish and so it would be difficult for

them to achieve surprise. Third, the Soviets correctly anticipated the German tactics of encirclement and annihilation and so strengthened the 16th and 50th Armies on each flank. Fourth, Stalin had agreed to the transfer of 15 divisions from the Far East as his intelligence indicated that Japan was getting ready to strike the Pacific, not the eastern Soviet Union.

The final German attack was launched on 15 November with 3rd and 4th Panzer Groups attacking from the north and 2nd Panzer striking to the south, while the 4th Army fixed Soviet forces in the centre. Even at this point, the Germans came very close to breaking through but, with the temperature down to around -35°C, the final attack by the 4th Army was halted on 4 December. Zhukov immediately counter-attacked and pushed the Germans away from the Soviet capital, almost encircling the 4th Army. At this point a crisis of confidence developed between Hitler and the German High Command with several field commanders being removed. The Soviets quickly tried to turn the local counter-attack at Moscow into an attempt to surround the whole of Army Group Centre but Stalin ordered an offensive along the entire front and the little strength that the Red Army had concentrated around Moscow was dissipated and the threat to Army Group Centre evaporated. By February 1942 the Soviet offensive had ground to a halt with little to show for it except around Moscow and south of Leningrad, where Army Group North came under intense pressure in the Lake Ilmen region during January 1942 and suffered heavy losses. Still, the Wehrmacht had regained its composure and Army Group South had even managed to take Rostov (temporarily as it turned out) and occupy most of the Crimea.

A German machinegun team with knocked-out Soviet tanks in the background. Timoshenko launched the Soviet offensive out of the Barvenkovo salient only a few days before Bock was due to launch Operation *Fridericus* and lost some 29 divisions and two-thirds of his tanks in the ensuing encirclement. (IWM, HU5165)

The narrow failure of Operation *Barbarossa* would mean that the Wehrmacht no longer had the strength and resources for another offensive on that sort of scale. By the end of January 1942, the Wehrmacht had suffered around one million casualties in the east, with Army Group South down to 50 per cent of their original infantry complement, while Army Groups North and Centre were both down to around 35 per cent. German AFV losses amounted to almost 4,200 and, by the end of March 1942, the 16 Panzer divisions on the Eastern Front were down to around 140 operational vehicles. The Wehrmacht also lost just over 100,000 motorized vehicles and just under 200,000 horses, which would seriously impact upon mobility and logistics.

Hitler, however, was unwilling just to stand on the defensive and consolidate the gains already made. What he needed was an offensive solution that with limited means would promise more than a limited result. With a broad-front offensive out of the question, he turned to the southern sector of the front (and thus wrong-footed the Soviets who expected a renewed offensive towards Moscow). If the Wehrmacht could capture the Caucasus oilfields, it would ensure the mobility of the Panzers and immobilize the Soviet armies. The Germans could then strike into the rear of the forces surrounding Moscow, or even at the new wartime industry concentrated in the Urals. Such an offensive, however, brought even greater risks than *Barbarossa*, as it would leave an exposed flank of 1,000 miles, along which it could be counter-attacked at any point.

An excellent view of part of a column of German infantry, showing the personal kit each man is carrying. They all have the M1939 A-Frame with the mess kit, battle-pack bag and shelter-quarter while the section machine-gunner also has his gas mask container strapped to it. The man behind is carrying a box of ammunition while the last in the group has a spare barrel. (Nik Cornish Library)

CHRONOLOGY

1939

28 August	Nazi-Soviet Non-Aggression Pact is signed by Molotov and Ribbentrop.
1 September	Germany invades Poland.
17 September	The Soviet Union occupies the territory agreed in the Nazi-Soviet Pact, including Eastern Poland and the Baltic States.

1940

18 December	Führer Directive No. 21 is issued, outlining Operation *Barbarossa*, the invasion of the USSR.

1941

14 June	Hitler clarifies *Barbarossa* objectives as being Leningrad, the Ukraine, Donbas and Caucasus. Moscow is not included.
22 June	Germany launches Operation *Barbarossa*.
19 July	Führer Directive No. 33 issued.
6 September	Führer Directive No. 35 (reinforcing Army Group Centre for the attack on Moscow) is issued.
30 September	Army Group Centre begins Operation *Typhoon*, the attack on Moscow.
5 December	Soviet counteroffensive before Moscow begins.

1942

5 April	Führer Directive No. 41 is issued, outlining the German summer offensive in southern Russia.
8 May	Von Manstein's 11th Army begins offensive operations in the Crimea.
12 May	Timoshenko launches the Soviet offensive towards Kharkov.
17 May	Army Group South begins counteroffensive towards Kharkov, eventually destroying three Soviet armies.
28 June	German summer offensive, Operation *Blau*, begins in the Kursk area.
4 July	Sevastopol falls.
6 July	Voronezh is captured by the Germans.
9 July	Army Group South is split into Army Groups A and B.
12 July	The Stalingrad Front is formed.
23 July	Germans capture Rostov. Führer Directive No. 45 states that Stalingrad and the Caucasus now have equal priority and are to be attacked simultaneously.
26 July	Army Group A begins its attack into the Caucasus.
4 August	German forces cross the Aksay river and start the drive on Stalingrad itself.
6 August	German forces cross the Kuban near Armavir.
9 August	The oilfield at Maykop falls to the Germans, who also take Krasnodar and Yeysk, a port on the Sea of Azov.
19 August	Paulus orders the 6th Army to advance on Stalingrad.
22 August	German advance into the Caucasus is temporarily halted.
26 August	Zhukov appointed Deputy Supreme Commander of the Soviet Armed Forces.
1 September	German and Rumanian troops cross the Kerch Straits and advance into the Taman Peninsula, establishing a bridgehead on the Terek.

3 September	6th Army reaches the outskirts of Stalingrad.
6 September	Novorossiysk on the Black Sea is captured by the Germans.
12 September	Chuikov takes control of 62nd Army.
14 September	The first German assault on Stalingrad begins as the 6th Army tries to force its way into the centre.
24 September	Germans begin advance towards Tuapse. Zeitzler replaces Halder as Chief of the Army General Staff.
27 September	The second German assault on the city begins.
6 October	Germans capture Malgobek.
14 October	The third German assault on the city starts.
18 October	German advance towards Tuapse halts.
19 November	The Soviets begin Operation *Uranus*, the offensive to encircle the 6th Army in Stalingrad.
20 November	Manstein is appointed commander of Army Group Don.
23 November	Soviet forces from the Southwestern and Stalingrad Fronts meet at Kalach, completing the encirclement of the 6th Army.

1943

13 January	Soviet counteroffensive in the Ukraine begins, codenamed Operation *Gallop*.
31 January	Paulus surrenders with the southern pocket.
2 February	The remaining German forces in the northern pocket surrender. The battle for Stalingrad is over. Soviets begin the second stage of their winter offensive, Operation *Star*.
16 February	Soviets retake Kharkov.
19 February	Von Manstein begins his counteroffensive, spearheaded by the SS Panzer Corps.
14 March	SS Panzer Corps retakes Kharkov.
5 July	Army Group Centre begins Operation *Zitadelle*.

1944

22 June	The Soviets launch Operation *Bagration*, the plan to destroy Army Group Centre in Byelorussia.
1 August	The Polish Home Army under General Komorowski rises in revolt and seizes large areas of Warsaw.
31 August	Germans finally retake Warsaw. The Soviet summer offensive comes to an end.

1945

12 January	Soviets begin their offensive from the Vistula to the Oder, with 1st Byelorussian Front reaching the river near Kustrin by mid-February.
16 April	The Soviets launch their offensive to take Berlin, led by Zhukov's 1st Byelorussian Front and Koniev's 1st Ukrainian Front.
30 April	Adolf Hitler and Eva Braun commit suicide.
1 May	Stalingrad is awarded 'Hero' city status.
2 May	The Berlin Garrison surrenders and the Soviets take the city.
8 May	German forces begin surrendering – the Western Allies declare VE Day.

1959

May	Construction begins of the memorial complex at Mamayev Kurgan.

1961

11 November	Stalingrad is renamed Volgograd.

1967

15 October	Memorial complex at Mamayev Kurgan is completed.

OPPOSING COMMANDERS

GERMAN

Generalfeldmarschall Fedor von Bock (1880–1945) was born in December 1880 in Küstrin, the son of a Prussian army officer. He became an officer cadet and passed out as a Leutnant in the 5th Regiment of Foot Guards. He was promoted to Hauptmann in 1912 and was on the General Staff during the First World War. During the inter-war years he remained in the army, gradually moving up the ranks, becoming a corps commander (as a Generaloberst) in 1935. He commanded the German forces that 'occupied' Austria in 1938 and played a role in the invasion of Czechoslovakia. He replaced von Rundstedt as an Army Group commander and led Army Group North to victory in the Polish campaign and Army Group B during the fighting for France and the Low Countries. He was promoted to Generalfeldmarschall and commanded Army Group Centre during Operation *Barbarossa*. He had to take sick leave for a stomach complaint but was back again in January 1942 to lead Army Group South but was retired by Hitler in July due to a number of disagreements. He took no more part in the war and he and his wife were killed by a low flying aircraft while travelling by car in North Germany in May 1945.

Generaloberst Freiherr Maximilian von Weichs (1881–1954) was born in Dessau on 12 November 1881 and joined the 2nd Bavarian Heavy Cavalry Regiment as a Fahnenjunker in July 1900. He was commissioned Leutnant in March 1902 and attended the War Academy

A Panzer IV of the Grossdeutschland Motorized Infantry Division, which, along with 24th Panzer Division, formed the XXXXVIII Panzer Corps, part of 4th Panzer Army led by Generaloberst Hermann Hoth. The division had started life in 1921 as a guard regiment in Berlin, but gradually expanded, eventually becoming a corps-sized unit in late 1944. (Nik Cornish Library)

in 1910. He was with the Bavarian Cavalry Division when the First World War broke out and held several General Staff appointments throughout the conflict. He was selected as one of the officers to stay on in the Reichswehr after the war and became a staff officer at the Infantry School in 1927. He had reached the rank of Oberst by 1930. Promoted to Generalmajor in 1933, he was given command of the 3rd Cavalry Division at Weimar, which became the 1st Panzer Division in 1935. He was promoted to Generalleutnant in April 1935 and then to General der Kavallerie in October 1936. He commanded XIII Corps during the invasion of Poland, followed by the 2nd Army (replacing Blaskowitz) during the battle for France. Promoted to Generaloberst and given the Knight's Cross in July 1940, he commanded the German forces invading northern Yugoslavia in April 1941 and then 2nd Army in Operation *Barbarossa*. He fell ill in November and did not return to duty until January 1941. He was given command of Army Group B when Army Group South was divided in two. He signalled his concern over the large number of non-German Axis formations in the army group and their ability to protect the flanks. After the Soviet counteroffensive of November 1942, most of his remaining forces were gradually transferred to Army Group Don or Army Group Centre and he was made a Generalfeldmarschall in February 1943. After being moved into the Führer Reserve in July 1943, he was quickly returned to duty as Commander-in-Chief, Southeast and in command of Army Group F. He had to contend with growing partisan activity and the Italian defection. With the break-up of the Axis in late 1944, he successfully withdrew all remaining German troops from the Balkans. He was finally retired in March 1945 and spent a short time as a PoW, appearing at the International War Crimes Tribunal but was released due to poor health. He died in Burg Rösberg (near Bonn) on 27 September 1954.

Generalfeldmarschall Wilhelm List (1880–1971) was born on 14 May 1880 in Oberkirchsberg. He served as a staff officer during World War One, joining the Freikorps afterwards and staying in the newly formed Reichswehr where he climbed the ranks, becoming a Generalmajor in

1930 and head of the Dresden Infantry School. Before the Nazis took power, List seemed to become more moderate in his political views and disciplined a number of young German officers for being too favourable towards the Nazi Party. He was privately critical of Hitler and the Nazis but became a Generaloberst in 1939, commanding the 14th Army during the invasion of Poland and 12th Army during the invasion of the Low Countries. He was promoted to Generalfeldmarschall in July 1940 and commanded the Axis forces in the Balkans area between June and October 1941. He was assigned the command of Army Group A on 9 July 1942 after Bock had been dismissed, only to be dismissed himself on 9 September 1942 for not making sufficient progress. He never held a command again and was arrested and tried for war crimes after the war. He was released in 1952 on the grounds of ill health and died on 17 August 1971.

A team of German medics inspect the wounds of a German soldier (whose face has been hidden so as not to be identified) before he is evacuated. By their sleeve insignia (a single chevron), the two orderlies in the middle and to the right are Sanitätsgefreiters (medical lance-corproals with six months' total service). (Nik Cornish Library)

General der Panzertruppen Friedrich Paulus (1890–1957) commanded the ill-fated 6th Army on the suggestion of Generalfeldmarschall Walter von Reichenau. An excellent staff officer, Paulus suffered the fate of being promoted beyond his experience and capabilities, due to his loyalty to the Führer. Born in Breitenau on 23 September 1890, he joined the army in 1910 and served in a number of staff positions during the First World War. After the war, Paulus remained in the Army and had reached the rank of Generalmajor by the outbreak of war in 1939. He served under Reichenau as Chief of Staff to the 10th Army and became Deputy Chief of the General Staff. After taking command of the 6th Army in January 1942, Paulus had to defend against Marshal Timoshenko's spring offensive and, after *Blau* began, advanced cautiously towards Stalingrad as his movement was restricted by fuel shortages. When he reached the city, he was drawn into an attritional urban battle. The army was surrounded by the Soviet counteroffensive of November 1942 and eventually surrendered in February 1943 after Paulus had been promoted to Generalfeldmarschall. Unlike Seydlitz-Kurzbach, Paulus did not initially cooperate with the Soviets but, after hearing that his friends Erich Hoepner and Erwin von Witzleben had been executed after the July Plot, he agreed to join the League of German Officers and make broadcasts calling for German officers and troops to surrender, desert or disobey orders. This resulted in the imprisonment of his family under Hitler's orders. He appeared as a witness for the Soviet Prosecution at the Nuremburg Trials in 1946 but was not released until 1953, his wife dying in Baden-Baden in 1949. He settled in Dresden, working for the East German Police but died on 1 February 1957.

GFM Friedrich Paulus soon after his surrender to the Soviets. An excellent staff officer, he was promoted above his ability and experience when he took over 6th Army. His decision to obey Hitler's 'stand fast' order condemned the army to certain destruction. (IWM, MH5646)

Generaloberst Freiherr (Baron) Wolfram von Richthofen was a cousin of the famous First World War fighter ace, Manfred von Richthofen, better known as the 'Red Baron', and was himself a fighter ace during the Great War. After the war he worked in engineering and then rejoined the Army in 1923, serving for a time as a military attaché in Rome. After transferring to the Luftwaffe, von Richthofen worked in the

Air Ministry after 1933 and in 1936 became an assistant to the head of the Technical Department. He briefly commanded the 'Kondor' Legion in Spain where, along with the campaigns in Poland, the Low Countries and France, he helped to perfect the tactical use of close-support aircraft, particularly the Ju-87 Stuka and, while sometimes critical of the Army, he never let it impede his performance. Göring rated him as one of his best operational commanders, alongside Kesselring. During the campaign he commanded Luftflotte IV which tried desperately to ferry supplies into the beleaguered 6th Army, despite his trying to make it clear that there were simply not enough transport assets available to move the kind of tonnages that were needed. He was promoted to Generalfeldmarschall on 17 February 1943 and was transferred back to the Mediterranean theatre from the Eastern Front. He retired on medical grounds in November 1944 and died of a brain tumour on 12 July 1945 while in captivity.

GenObst von Richthofen (in striped breeches) conferring with a staff officer during Operation *Blau*. It was his Luftflotte IV that had to fulfil Göring's boast that they could keep the 6th Army supplied by air, a mission von Richthofen knew to be virtually impossible. (Nik Cornish Library)

Generaloberst Hermann Hoth commanded the 4th Panzer Army during the campaign. Born in Neuruppen on 12 April 1891, the son of an Army medical officer, he joined the army in 1904 and served during the First World War in a variety of staff positions and as a battalion commander in the 342nd Infantry Regiment. After the war he remained in the Reichswehr and eventually rose to take command of the 18th Infantry Division at Liegnitz in 1935 as a Generalmajor. In 1938 he was promoted to Generalleutnant and took command of the XV Corps, a formation which he commanded as a General der Infanterie during the campaign for France and the Low Countries. He was promoted to Generaloberst and during Operation *Barbarossa* he led Panzergruppe 3 which helped to encircle hundreds of thousands of Soviet troops in the Vyazma-Bryansk pocket. He commanded 17th Army for a period of time but was given command of the 4th Panzer Army in May 1942. After Stalingrad, he took part in the battles for Kharkov and Kursk but was made a scapegoat for some of Hitler's bad decisions and was retired in December 1943. He died on 26 January 1971.

GenObst von Kleist, shown here just after his capture by American troops. He commanded 1st Panzer Army during the Caucasus campaign and, after the disaster at Stalingrad, led a successful retreat to the Dniepr. (IWM, EA63009)

Generaloberst Ewald von Kleist was born on 8 August 1881 in Brauenfels and joined the artillery in 1900 as an officer cadet. He went to the War Academy and served with distinction during the First World War, teaching at the Cavalry School in Hanover after the war. By 1936 he had been promoted to General der Kavallerie. Retired in February 1938 as part of the purges, he was recalled to duty and commanded XXII Corps during the Polish campaign and a Panzergruppe during the campaign in France, where he led it through the Ardennes to the English Channel and then south to the Spanish border. He received the Knight's Cross and a promotion to Generaloberst. He then led his Panzergruppe into the Balkans to take part in the Yugoslav campaign.

Barbarossa followed, where his Panzergruppe was part of Army Group South, taking part in the surrounding of Kiev, the taking of Rostov and halting Timoshenko's spring offensive, after which he received his oak leaves. After the Caucasus campaign he was promoted to Generalfeldmarschall, conducted a brilliant withdrawal back to the Dnieper and maintained a defence of the Kuban bridgehead. He was not allowed to withdraw his forces in the Crimea and they were eventually cut off, but he allowed General Wöhler to withdraw behind the Dniester river. For this he was sacked after being given his swords to the Knight's Cross by Hitler. He spent the rest of the war in retirement but had to evacuate his family to Bavaria due to the advancing Soviets. After spending time in Britain as a PoW, he was extradited to Yugoslavia and then moved to the Soviet Union where he was sentenced to life imprisonment for alleged war crimes. He died on 16 October 1954 at Vladimir PoW Camp, near Moscow.

GFM Erich von Manstein was given command of Army Group Don to try and relieve the encircled 6th Army at Stalingrad during Operation Winter Storm. He managed to get within thirty miles of the city despite fierce Soviet resistance. (IWM, MH2104)

Generalfeldmarschall Erich von Manstein – was actually born Erich von Lewinski on 24 November 1887 in Berlin but was brought up and adopted by an aunt and uncle. He joined the Army in 1906 and had reached the rank of Oberleutnant by the time the First World War had broken out and served in a variety of staff posts, after being badly wounded in November 1914. He remained in the Army after the war and by 1937 had reached the rank of Generalmajor. At the outbreak of the Second World War he was Chief of Staff to von Rundstedt's Army Group South but quickly came to prominence with the idea of attacking through the Ardennes to circumvent the Maginot Line. Hitler eventually adopted the plan and he was given command of the XXXVIII Corps during the campaign. He was awarded the Knight's Cross and promoted to General der Infanterie, commanding LVI Panzer Corps at the start of Operation *Barbarossa*. He was then given command of the 11th Army in late 1941 and eventually managed to capture the fortress at Sebastopol in July 1942, for which he was promoted to Generalfeldmarschall. He led the counteroffensive by Army Group Don to relieve the 6th Army at Stalingrad and managed to get within 30 miles of the city but was forced back. With the Soviets now on the offensive, he conducted a series of brilliant defensive battles at Krasnograd, Kharkov and Belgorod. He continually argued with Hitler over strategy and was finally dismissed in March 1944, never having another command. He was charged with war crimes before a British court in 1949 and was sentenced to 18 years' imprisonment. His defence was paid for by a group of British officers who disagreed with the decision but he only served three years due to medical reasons. He died on 11 June 1973 after writing two books.

GenLt Werner Sanne, commander of the 100th Jäger Division, surrendering to Soviet forces, 31 January 1943. He had commanded the division since December 1940, before which he had led the 34th Infantry Division. He spent the rest of his life in Soviet captivity, dying in 1952 at the Krasnopdic PoW Camp. (IWM, FLM1499)

General der Artillerie Walther von Seydlitz-Kurzbach (1888–1976) commanded LI Corps during the battle for Stalingrad. He was born in Hamburg-Eppendorf on 22 August 1888 and was related to General Friedrich Wilhelm von Seydlitz, a cavalry commander under Frederick the Great. He joined the army and, after attending the War Academy at Hanover, he initially served on the Eastern Front during the First World War. He was badly wounded at the battle of Gumbinnen and, after recovering, fought at the Somme, Passchendaele, St Quentin and in Ludendorff's spring offensive of 1918. He stayed in the Army after the

war, working in the Reichswehr Ministry from 1929 until 1933, where he was promoted to Major. After the outbreak of the Second World War he was promoted to Generalmajor and took command of the 12th Infantry Division at Mecklenberg. The division took part in the battle for France, but remained on occupation duty in both France and the Netherlands until it was transferred east to take part in Operation *Barbarossa*. The division performed well and Seydlitz-Kurzbach was awarded his oak leaves to the Knight's Cross earned in France, as well as being promoted to Generalleutnant. He was next involved in the relief of the Demyansk Pocket and was promoted to General der Artillerie in June 1942 after taking command of LI Corps. As Stalingrad gradually drew in the 6th Army, Seydlitz-Kurzbach saw a major trap in the making and warned Paulus to withdraw from the costly battle – advice that was ignored. He was captured at Stalingrad on 31 January 1943 and, being extremely disillusioned and suffering mental instability over the débâcle at Stalingrad, he and a number of other German officers formed the League of German Officers, a military equivalent to the National Free Germany Committee. The League was intended to help persuade German officers and troops that were surrounded to surrender, but it was a failure. He was sentenced to death by a military tribunal on 26 April 1944 and his wife was persuaded to divorce him for the sake of their own safety. After being kept in various prison camps and put on a show trial, he returned to Germany in October 1955, together with about 2,000 other German soldiers captured at Stalingrad, and was reunited with his family. The death sentence was overturned in 1956 and he lived in obscure retirement until his death on 28 April 1976.

GenMaj Hubert Lanz and the staff of 1st Gebirgs Division planning the next move during the division's advance towards the Caucasus alongside 4th Gebirgs Division. Members of the Gebirgsjäger even managed to plant the German flag on top of Mount Elbrus, the highest peak in the Caucasus Mountains. (Nik Cornish Library)

SOVIET

General Georgi K. Zhukov (1896–1974) was conscripted into the Imperial Russian Army in 1915 but joined the Red Army in 1918 and the Communist Party in 1919. By 1938 he had risen to the post of Deputy Commander, Byelorussian Military District and was sent to repel the Japanese incursion into Mongolia. He was then promoted to full general and given the command of the Kiev Special Military District, followed by Chief of the General Staff and Deputy Minister of Defence. Given command of the Leningrad Front, he stopped the German advance at the gates of the city, after which he coordinated the defence of Moscow, the battle for Stalingrad and went on to play a key role in the battle for Kursk. He was promoted to a Marshal of the Soviet Union in 1943, commanded the 1st Ukrainian Front in early 1944 and led Operation *Bagration* in June. He commanded the 1st Byelorussian Front during the drive across Poland and the assault on Berlin. After the war he remained as Commander, Group of Soviet Forces Germany until March 1946 and commanded the Odessa and Ural Military Districts after a short period as a Deputy Minister of Defence. It is rumoured that Zhukov (along with Koniev) played a role in the arrest of Lavrentii Beria (Head of the NKVD) and supported Khrushchev during his attempted removal in June 1957. He had however significant disagreements with Khrushchev over defence policy and was removed from office later that year. He died on 18 June 1974.

General Alexandr M. Vasilevsky (1895–1977) had served in the Russian Army during the First World War and joined the Red Army in 1919. After becoming a regimental commander, he joined the General Staff in 1940 and became head of its Operational Directorate (War Planning). In June 1942 he was appointed Deputy Chief of the General Staff and a Deputy Minister of Defence (also known as a People's Commissar) but had an influential involvement with the counteroffensive at Stalingrad, coordinated the movements of several fronts during the battle for Kursk and was actually wounded during the fighting around Sebastopol. He was promoted to marshal in 1943 and awarded the Hero of the Soviet Union twice (July 1944 and May 1945). After the war in Europe had ended, he became Commander-in-Chief of the Soviet Forces in the Far East, controlling three fronts during the invasion of Manchuria in the final days of the Second World War. After the war he remained Chief of the General Staff and became Defence Minister between 1949 and 1953. He lost influence after Khrushchev came to power, eventually retired and he died on 5 December 1977.

Colonel General Andrei I. Yeremenko (1892–1970) was born in Markovka (near Kharkov) to a peasant family. He was drafted into the Imperial Army in 1913, serving on the Southwest and Romanian fronts during the First World War but joined the Red Army in 1918, where he served in the legendary 'Budyonny Cavalry' unit, after which he attended the Leningrad Cavalry School and then the Frunze Military Academy, which he graduated from in 1935. Yeremenko commanded the 6th Cavalry Corps during the invasion and partition of Poland and by 1941 was commanding the Transbaikal Military District, but was recalled by Stalin after the Germans invaded and given command of first, the Western Front and then the Bryansk Front. He led a counter-attack which stalled the German drive on Moscow, thus helping to save the city, and contributed to the defence of Stalingrad as commander of the Southeastern Front (which was renamed Stalingrad Front, then Southern Front). Command of various formations followed as did action in the Caucasus, Crimea, the Baltic and Hungary. In May 1945 his 4th Ukrainian Front surrounded Army Group Centre in conjunction with Koniev's 1st Ukrainian Front. After the war he commanded three military districts (Carpathia, Western Siberia and North Caucasus), retiring in 1958.

Konstantin K. Rokossovsky (1896–1968) was a former Tsarist cavalry NCO who joined the Red Army in 1918. He was imprisoned during the purges but released in March 1940 after the Russo-Finnish War on the orders of Stalin himself. He was seriously wounded during the fighting around Moscow, but returned to duty in September 1942 just in time to take part in the battle for Stalingrad, where he commanded the Stalingrad Front, eventually renamed the Don Front. After Stalingrad, the Don Front was renamed the Central Front and took part in the battle for Kursk. He then went on to command a number of fronts until the end of the war, including the 2nd Byelorussian during the assault on Berlin. After the war he went on to

Konstantin Rokossovsky, here with FM Bernard Montgomery, commanded the Stalingrad Front during the battle and led the final assault on the besieged 6th Army. He went on to command the Central Front during the battle of Kursk and the 2nd Byelorussian Front during the battle for Berlin. (IWM, BU5523)

hold the posts of Deputy Minister of Defence and Inspector General of the Ministry of Defence, and returned to Poland (he was Polish by birth) as Minister of National Defence between 1949 and 1956. He eventually returned to the USSR and was appointed a Deputy Minister of Defence. He retired in 1962 and died on 3 August 1968.

General Nikolai F. Vatutin (1901–1944) commanded the Southwest Front during the battle. He was born in Chepukhino, near Valuiki, in the province of Voronezh. He joined the Red Army in 1920 and attended a command course in Poltava after which he attended the Kiev Higher Formation Military School (1924) and eventually entered the Frunze Military Academy in 1926 and again in 1934. In 1937 he received an appointment as Assistant Chief of Staff in the Kiev Special Military District and later, First Deputy Chief of the General Staff with responsibility for mobilization and deployment. After Barbarossa, Vatutin took command of the Northern Front and delayed the German advance on Leningrad. He then served as Deputy Chief of the General Staff under Vasilevsky and was then appointed as a Stavka representative to the Bryansk Front, quickly followed by command of the Voronezh Front in July 1942. In October, Vatutin was summoned to Moscow and given command of the Southwest Front that took part in the Soviet counteroffensive at Stalingrad. He was again placed in command of the Voronezh Front in March 1943, taking part in the battle for Kursk. His front was renamed the 1st Ukrainian Front and took part in the advance to the Dnieper and the liberation of Kiev. During the Soviet winter offensive in the Ukraine, Vatutin, his Chief of Staff, K. Kraynyukov and a security detachment of ten men were travelling between the 13th Army HQ at Rovno and the 60th Army HQ at Slavata when they were ambushed by Ukrainian partisans. Vatutin was wounded in the leg and subsequently died of his wounds on 15 April 1944.

General Vasily I. Chuikov (1900–1982) joined the Red Army in 1919 and rose through the ranks quickly, mainly due to his membership of the Communist Party. He attended the Frunze Military Academy, took part in the Soviet occupation of eastern Poland, the Russo-Finnish War and served as a military adviser to Chiang Kai-shek. In May 1942 he was recalled and eventually placed in command of the 62nd Army, which defended Stalingrad. He was then promoted to command the 8th Guards Army, which he led for the rest of the war. Afterwards he served as Commander, Group of Soviet Forces Germany from 1949 until 1953, commanded the Kiev Military District and, after having been made a Marshal of the Soviet Union in 1955, was appointed Commander-in-Chief of the Soviet Ground Forces between 1960 and 1964. He retired from the armed forces in 1972 and after his death on 18 March 1982 became the first marshal to be buried outside Moscow, in the memorial complex at Mamayev Kurgan.

OPPOSING FORCES

GERMAN FORCES

Operation *Blau* was to be undertaken by Army Group South, under the command of GFM Fedor von Bock, while Centre and North remained on the defensive. In 1942, the Wehrmacht was no longer in a position to be able to undertake simultaneous offensives by all three army groups. Despite receiving over 1.1 million replacements up to May 1942, the German Army still had a shortfall of about 625,000 personnel. Army Group South therefore had the priority on replacements and reinforcement formations being moved from the west and the other two army groups had their Panzer forces cannibalized in order to bring Army Group South up to full strength. In early May, GenMaj Hans von Greiffenberg, who had been Bock's Chief of Staff at Army Group Centre and was due to become Chief of Staff under GFM Wilhelm List at Army Group A, started to assemble the army group staff at the OKH compound in Zossen, just south of Berlin. Two weeks later he took a detachment to the Army Group South headquarters at Poltava and despatched a forward element to Stalino. Until it became operational, the headquarters would go under the cover name of 'Coastal Staff, Azov' to preserve secrecy, which extended to the other major formation head-quarters moving into the area.

By the eve of Operation *Blau*, Army Group South disposed of 45 infantry, 11 Panzer, four light infantry and five motorized divisions. There were also the 8th Italian (Garibaldi), 2nd Hungarian (Jany), 3rd Romanian (Dumitrescu) and 4th Romanian (Constantinescu) Armies available and these totalled some 25 divisions. While this was technically five more than Bock had estimated he would need, the Axis divisions could not be counted as fully equivalent to a German division for a variety of reasons including equipment, training, leadership and morale. One solution to the manpower shortage had been for Berlin to secure an increase in the numbers of Axis satellite troops to complement the German forces on the Eastern Front, a solution actively sought in early 1942. By the time of the battle for Stalingrad, Axis forces had increased to 24 Rumanian, ten Italian and ten Hungarian divisions serving in the east. Most of these divisions formed the Axis

A German Leutnant, seen here with a captured PPSh41, a Soviet sub-machinegun designed by Georgii Shpagin. It was simple, crudely finished but effective, with a high rate of fire and large magazine capacity. Over 5 million were made and a number were employed by the Germans, some being converted to 9mm. (IWM, HU5139)

A German machinegun team with a Stug III nearby. Deployed primarily in infantry formations, it was based on the Panzer III chassis and started out as a light close-support gun. It was continuously upgraded throughout the war until it had become a tank destroyer. Over 10,000 were built. (IWM, HU5159)

A 7.5cm Gebirgskanone and crew. On the steppe, these weapons could be towed by trucks, half-tracks or horses. If, however, the mountain troops went into rough terrain these weapons could be quickly disassembled into several component parts and transported by mules. (Nik Cornish Library)

contingents on the Don that were eventually to protect the flanks of the 6th Army but the German reliance on such large allied forces in such a vulnerable area was to have dire consequences. Even so, while not of comparable quality to German formations, they were a useful strategic asset as they released German forces to undertake mobile offensive operations but had to be reinforced with German units when facing a Soviet attack.

Army Group South was, therefore, a powerful force, with over one million German and 300,000 Axis troops and would be supported from

the air by Luftflotte IV under GenObst Wolfram von Richthofen. The Panzer divisions had spaces for over 1,900 tanks but, as they would be refitted at or near to the front and some were in action before the start of the campaign proper, the exact numbers of serviceable tanks is almost impossible to calculate. The Panzer divisions were, however, being refitted with tanks that carried long-barrelled guns (the Panzer III having the 50mm and Panzer IV having the 75mm) that could penetrate the T-34 from all angles (although in the case of the Panzer III, it would have to wait until the target was within 400 yards). The output of 75mm heavy anti-tank guns had been unexpectedly high, so many of these would be deployed in the infantry formations, particularly the 2nd Army which would be holding the front near Voronezh. The only hitch was that the output of armour-piercing ammunition would not catch up until mid-summer and so the number of rounds per gun would have to be severely limited with only 70 to 150 rounds for anti-tank guns and 30 to 50 rounds for the Panzer IVs. The crews would have to be very sparing in their use of this ammunition. The 2nd Army even issued instructions that the 75mm guns should only be used for head-on shots. If the T-34 showed its flanks or rear, the 50mm guns should be used.

Soon after the start of the main campaign, Army Group South would split into two separate army groups, Army Group A (Bock, then List) comprising the 1st and 4th Panzer Armies and 17th Army with around 40 divisions and Army Group B (Weichs) comprising the German 2nd and 6th Armies supported by the Italian, Hungarian and Rumanian armies with around 50 divisions. A study by the OKH Organisation Branch (conducted concurrently with the broader OKW analysis of overall Wehrmacht strength) of Army Group South's readiness to conduct the summer campaign revealed that, whereas all the divisions of one type could be relied upon to be virtually identical in terms of combat effectiveness, the losses incurred during *Barbarossa* and the Soviet winter counteroffensive meant that this would no longer be true.

German infantry resting in a trench with a dead soldier in the foreground. Blitzkrieg on the Russian steppes meant long periods of marching with shorter, more intense periods of combat, followed by more marching, which was very wearing on men and equipment. (IWM, HU5147)

Given that many of the divisions scheduled to take part in the operation would have to be rebuilt to some degree, they would necessarily fall into one of three categories. The first category would be 15 infantry and six Panzer and motorized divisions that would have just been transferred to or fully rebuilt behind the front. They would be at full strength and would have time to let the experienced troops rest and allow the replacements to settle in. The second category consisted of 17 infantry divisions and ten Panzer and motorized divisions who would be at full strength but, because they would be rebuilt near the front, there would not be time to rest and properly integrate the replacements. The third category would include 17 infantry divisions (more than a quarter of the total) that would neither be fully rested nor rebuilt. The formations would be 'approximately' at full strength in terms of total personnel and equipment but would be short of officers and non-commissioned officers, at least for the start of the operation.

However, it was noticeable that in all three categories some corners would have to be cut. The infantry divisions' supply trains would be horse-drawn and every division would have to take 1,000 of the newest and greenest recruits (18 and 19-year-old troops who had just completed their basic training). The Panzer and motorized divisions would also have fewer tracked armoured personnel carriers, reaching about 80 per cent of full mobility, but even this would entail some use of trucks and therefore some reduction in cross-country performance. In the Panzer divisions, the rifle battalions would be reduced from five to four companies. Since there was very little in reserve, much of the replacement equipment would be coming from scheduled production, which meant that current schedules could not be accelerated or production increased until the campaign was well underway and any unanticipated loss in the preliminary operations would not be able to be replaced. Army Group South looked at the same divisions and came to the conclusion that 'owing to diverse composition, partial lack of battle experience and gaps in their outfitting, the units available for the summer operation in 1942 will not have the combat effectiveness that could be taken for granted at the beginning of the campaign in the East. The mobile units, too, will not have the flexibility, the endurance, or the penetrating power they had a year ago.'

THE GERMAN ORDER OF BATTLE

Army Group A – GFM Wilhelm List (until 9 Sept 1942)

1st Panzer Army – GenObst Ewald von Kleist
17th Army – Gen d.Inf Richard Ruoff

Army Group B - GenObst Freiherr Maximilian von Weichs

2nd Army – Gen Hans von Salmuth
Hungarian 2nd Army – ColGen Gusztav Jany
Italian 8th Army – Generale d'Armata Italo Gariboldi
Rumanian 3rd Army – Gen Petre Dumitrescu
4th Panzer Army – GenObst Hermann Hoth
      XXXXVIII Panzer Corps – GenLt Ferdinand Heim
      Rumanian VI Corps
      Rumanian VII Corps
(These last two were in the process of being transferred to the Rumanian 4th Army under Gen C. Constantinescu.)

6th Army – Gen d.Pnztpn Friedrich Paulus
    4th, 46th, 64th & 70th Artillery Regiments
    54th, 616th, 627th & 849th Artillery Battalions
    49th, 101st & 733rd Heavy Artillery Battalions
    51st & 53rd Mortar Regiments
    2nd & 30th Nebelwerter Regiments

    IV Corps – Gen d.Pioniere Erwin Jaenecke
            29th Motorized Infantry Division – Leyser
            297th Infantry Division – Pfeffer
            371st Infantry Division – Stempel
    VIII Corps – Gen d.Art Walther Heitz
            76th Infantry Division – Rodenburg
            113th Infantry Division – von Arnim
    XI Corps – GenLt Karl Strecker
            44th Infantry Division – Deboi
            376th Infantry Division – von Daniels
            384th Infantry Division – von Gablenz
    XIV Panzer Corps – Gen d.Pztpn Hans Hube
            3rd Motorized Infantry Division – Schlomer
            60th Motorized Infantry Division – Kohlermann
            16th Panzer Division – Angern
    LI Corps - Gen d.Art Walther von Seydlitz-Kurzbach
            71st Infantry Division – von Hartmann
            79th Infantry Division – von Schwerin
            94th Infantry Division – Pfeiffer
            100th Jäger Division – Sanne
                (with 369th Croatian Regiment)
            295th Infantry Division – Korfes
            305th Infantry Division – Steinmetz
            389th Infantry Division – Magnus
            14th Panzer Division – Lattmann
            24th Panzer Division – von Lenski
    9th Flak Division – GenLt Wolfgang Pickert

Luftwaffe Air Support

Luftflotte IV - GenObst Freiherr Wolfram von Richthofen
    Fliegerkorps IV – GenLt Kurt Pflugbeil
    Fliegerkorps VIII – GenLt Martin Fiebig

SOVIET FORCES

The Red Army had been effectively decapitated just before the outbreak of the Second World War by the Great Purge enacted by Stalin, whose paranoia sought to eliminate any potential threat to his hold on power. At least 30,000 officers were imprisoned, tortured or executed with the victims including three out of the five marshals and 14 out of the 16 army commanders. The consequences of this were, first, the Red Army just barely winning the Russo-Finnish War, fought between November 1939 and March 1940 and, second, the near-disaster at the hands of the Wehrmacht during Operation *Barbarossa*.

By the summer of 1942, the Red Army had barely survived the Wehrmacht's onslaught and, after pushing the Germans away from Moscow, prepared for a renewed onslaught after the initiative had once again passed to the Germans. The primary Soviet commands in the area of *Blau* were the Bryansk (Golikov), Southwest (Timoshenko), South (Malinovsky) and North Caucasus (Budenny) fronts. The first three had

Soviet soldiers advance into the dust and smoke created by an artillery bombardment. In such conditions, both sides relied heavily on the initiative and leadership of their junior commanders, which was easier for the Germans than the Soviets. (IWM, RR1425)

been under the Southwestern Theatre Command but this had ceased to operate as an effective headquarters and was abolished at the start of June as Timoshenko and his staff had been fully engaged with operations by the Southwest Front during May and June. In addition, Stalin had told Timoshenko and Bagramyan that the Bryansk Front would not be part of the theatre for much longer and so was effectively under Stavka control. The four fronts had a total of 17 field armies, with Southwest, South and Bryansk having five each and North Caucasus having just two. Each had an air army attached to it and the Bryansk Front, having 5th Tank Army in reserve, gave up 61st Army to West Front on 29 June. In the first week of June, Army Group South estimated that it would have to deal with 91 Soviet rifle divisions, 32 rifle brigades, 20 cavalry divisions and 44 tank brigades. As it happens, this was not too far off the mark, with the Bryansk, Southwest and South fronts having approximately 81 rifle divisions, 38 brigades, 12 cavalry divisions and 62 tank brigades

Romanian mountain troops in the foothills of the Caucasus Mountains. The Romanian Mountain Corps had only been formed after the First World War but quickly established itself as an elite organisation. Four mountain divisions (1st, 2nd, 3rd and 4th) fought in the Crimea and Caucasus as part of the 11th and 1st Panzer Armies. (Nik Cornish Library)

with a published strength of 1.7 million men and 2,300 tanks. However, the number of tanks in each brigade was approximately 60 tanks per formation, as the actual strength of the tank corps in the Bryansk Front in June 1942 was 24 KVs, 88 T-34s and 68 T-60s for a total of 180 tanks in three brigades. This would give an overall tank strength of 3,720 so the published figures presumably do not include the T-60s in each brigade.

Army Group South estimated that another 36 rifle divisions, 16 rifle brigades, seven cavalry divisions and ten tank brigades were deployed in the Caucasus. The true picture appears to be 17 rifle divisions, three rifle brigades, three cavalry divisions and three tank brigades. These figures, however, do not include the available Stavka reserves, which included four reserve armies situated behind the Don to the rear of the Bryansk and Southwest Fronts, at Stalingrad, Tambov, Novokhopersk and Novosnninsky, with another two behind them. Of the four fronts, the Bryansk was considered by the Soviets to be the most strategically important as its right flank, to the north and east of Orel, covered the Tula approach to Moscow, while its left flank covered the approach to Voronezh. Both Kazakov and Vasilevsky have said that of the two, the former was considered the more likely avenue of attack. This was due to the fact that both Stalin and Stavka expected the Germans to renew their attack towards Moscow, then considered still the most important Soviet target, that Army Group Centre still consisted of over 70 divisions, some of which were less than 100 miles from the city, and that the Germans had instituted a deception plan to cover Operation *Blau*, codenamed Operation *Kreml*, to indicate that they were preparing another summer offensive by Army Group Centre towards the capital.

On 23 April, Stavka ordered Golikov to prepare an attack towards Orel to coincide with Timoshenko's offensive to retake Kharkov. Golikov could not get his forces ready in time and, after the German counter-attack had begun, had all his air support diverted south to help Timoshenko's Southwest Front. For this particular operation, Golikov had been given four rifle divisions, five tank and two cavalry corps and four tank brigades out of the Stavka reserve but after the disaster in the Barvenkovo Salient, he was tasked with preparing to counter-attack in whichever direction the Germans decided to launch their summer offensive. By late June, Golikov had amassed four rifle divisions, four tank brigades, two cavalry corps and six tank corps with a total of 1,640 tanks. These consisted of 191 KVs, 650 T-34s and 799 T-60s and older models. The one problem Golikov, and indeed most other front and army commanders had, was that Stavka had activated the tank formations without giving anyone any guidance on how they might be employed. He had stationed his reserves to meet the two possible thrusts with 5th Tank Army and VIII Cavalry Corps near Chern on the Orel–Tula road, VII Cavalry Corps and two tank brigades just north of their position and I, XVI and IV Tank Corps placed on the left flank facing Kursk. Despite the intelligence gleaned from a crashed Luftwaffe aircraft carrying a staff officer from the 23rd Panzer Division, Maj Joachim Reichel, who had been carrying the plans for the opening phase of Operation *Blau* and reports from air reconnaissance of an enemy build-up, Stalin ordered Golikov to prepare for an offensive towards Orel timed for 5 July, a plan Golikov and his staff finished drafting in the early hours of 28 June. A few hours later, Operation *Blau* began.

THE SOVIET ORDER OF BATTLE

Stavka

Gen Georgi K. Zhukov
ColGen Aleksandr M. Vasilevsky

Voronezh Front – Gen Filip I. Golikov

Transcaucasus Front – Gen Ivan V. Tyulenev

Southwest Front – Gen Nikolay F. Vatutin
    63rd Army – Gen Fyodor I. Kuznetsov
    21st Army – MajGen I.M. Christyakov
    5th Tank Army – LtGen P.L. Romanenko
    1st Guards Army – LtGen Dimitri D. Lelyushenko

    2nd Air Army
    17th Air Army – Krasovsky

Don Front - ColGen Konstantin K. Rokossovsky
    66th Army – MajGen A.S. Zhadov
    24th Army – Gen I.V. Galinin
    65th Army – LtGen Pavel I. Batov

    16th Air Army – Rudenko

Stalingrad Front – ColGen Andrei I. Yeremenko
    64th Army – Gen Mikhail S. Shumilov
    57th Army – LtGen Fydor I. Tolbukhin
    51st Army – Gen N.I. Trufanov
    28th Army – LtGen D.I. Ryabyshev
    62nd Army – LtGen Vasily I. Chuikov
        10th NKVD Rifle Division – Sarayev
        13th Guards Rifle Division – Rodimtsev
        35th Guards Rifle Division – Dubyanski
        37th Guards Rifle Division – Zholudev
        39th Guards Rifle Division – Guriev
        45th Rifle Division – Sokolov
        95th Rifle Division – Gorishny
        112th Rifle Division – Solugub
        138th Rifle Division – Lyudnikov
        193rd Rifle Division – Smekhotvorov
        196th Rifle Division – Ivanov
        244th Rifle Division – Afanasiev
        284th Rifle Division – Batyuk
        308th Rifle Division – Gurtiev
        92nd Naval Infantry Brigade – Samodai
        42nd, 115th, 124th, 149th & 160th Special Brigades
        84th, 137th & 189th Tank Brigades

8th Air Army – Khryukin

OPPOSING PLANS

GERMAN

After the failure of *Barbarossa*, Germany found herself at war with not only the USSR, which, despite the damage inflicted on it the previous year, still had the largest army in the world, but also with Great Britain, which had the largest empire in the world, and the United States, which was the greatest economic power in the world. Hitler knew that this was a coalition that Germany did not have the manpower or economic resources to defeat in a prolonged war and so it was vital that Germany knock the Soviet Union out of the war in 1942, gaining her agricultural and industrial assets with which to meet the Western Allies head on.

In Führer Directive No. 41 of 5 April 1942, Hitler laid out how this was to be accomplished. The target for the new offensive would be the Soviet forces in the south and the Soviet oilfields in the southern Caucasus, around Maykop, Grozny and Baku. Given Germany's remaining stocks of oil, it could not sustain another offensive on the scale of *Barbarossa*, let alone a prolonged war of attrition against the Allied coalition. Whatever they might have thought privately, publicly few German generals (with the exception of Halder) questioned the designation of oil as the main objective for the 1942 summer offensive, although their main concern was still the destruction of the Red Army. After the war, many blamed Hitler for the failure of the 1942 offensive but this was more to do with the German approach to war, rather than just Hitler's approach to it. Like the plan for *Barbarossa* (Directive 21), Directive 41 was a statement of German strategy, rather than a detailed planning document and covered just the first phase of operations that saw the destruction of the Red Army south of the Don river through a series of encirclements.

At this point, Stalingrad was a secondary objective to the capture of the Caucasus oilfields and the destruction of the Red Army in the south. Operation *Blau*, as it was conceived, was to have four stages. The first stage would see a powerful drive eastwards from the area around Kursk by the 4th Panzer and 2nd Armies under von Weichs. The second stage would see the 6th Army advance to reach the banks of the Don river in the vicinity of Voronezh and encircle the Red Army to the west of the river. The third stage would see 4th Panzer Army moving south-east following the Don to trap and eliminate those Red Army formations that had been driven east by the 17th Army advancing east from Rostov. German forces would then cut the Volga river north of Stalingrad and then receive orders for the Caucasus campaign, the objectives being Maykop, Grozny and a rapid advance down the Volga south of Stalingrad to Baku. As a prelude to Operation *Blau*, Army Group South were to undertake some preparatory movements to secure jumping-off points,

German troops in a foxhole, in front of a knocked-out KV-1 tank. The KV series of heavy tanks proved to be formidable opponents in the early stages of the campaign on the Eastern Front as they had heavy armour that the Germans found difficult to penetrate except at close range. (IWM, HU5160)

including the elimination of the Soviet forces remaining in the Crimea and that of the Barvenkovo salient.

It seemed, however, that German planning for the 1942 offensive bore some ominous similarities to that of *Barbarossa* the year before. In the initial attack upon the Soviet Union, the Germans fielded over three million men, looking for a strategic military victory in a single campaign (*Vernichtungsschlacht*). Due to the lack of an operational campaign plan, squandered time and resources in tactical encounters (brilliantly executed though they were), the overall goal of winning the war in the east in a single blow remained elusive. While it was doubtful if the Germans had really had the means to achieve their ends in 1941, it was even more questionable now. The Germans just managed to hold their lines together during the Soviet winter counteroffensive but now, with fewer troops, Hitler envisaged the conquest and occupation of another massive area. Additionally, the roads leading south to the Caucasus would be inferior to even the poor roads found in the western USSR and the Germans were for the moment still heavily dependent on movement and supply over the road network as the railways consisted only of a few single lines running east and south. The 1942 campaign would be continually hindered by the problem of supply. Also, as in 1941, the objective of the campaign was to acquire the resources to fight a long war in the west but this in effect undermined the German chances of winning the war in the east quickly. If it was to have succeeded, the Wehrmacht should have gone for an objective that would have achieved this – either the destruction of the Red Army or the capture of Moscow. Even if the Wehrmacht had executed its campaign perfectly and achieved the objectives set out for Operation *Blau*, the Soviets would have suffered a massive blow, but given there were oilfields near the Ural Mountains and to the east of the Caspian Sea, and the will of the Soviets to continue the fight, it is doubtful whether this would have achieved the complete defeat of the Soviet Union.

SOVIET

The chief priority for the USSR at the beginning of 1942 was to take advantage of its new strategic alliance with Great Britain and the United States and to repair its shattered war economy. Amazingly, the Soviets had managed to move around 1,500 of its most vital war industries, in the face of the German advance, to locations near the Ural Mountains and in the eastern Soviet Union. These industries, however, would have to be unloaded and put back together before any new production could be undertaken. It was glaringly obvious that the devastated Red Army would need to be re-trained and re-equipped under new commanders if it was even to hold its own against the Wehrmacht, let alone consider taking the offensive and liberating those lands under German control. The Red Army had substantial manpower reserves but they were not infinite and could not cope with further losses and defeats on the scale of 1941.

Strategy was planned by the Soviet High Command (otherwise known as the Stavka) but Stalin played an overarching, dictatorial role – once his mind was made up, that was that. Not even Zhukov could change it. On 5 January 1942 following the successful defence of Moscow, Zhukov was summoned to a meeting at Stavka during which future operations were being discussed. Stalin put forward a plan for a general offensive from Leningrad to the Black Sea. Aware that, while Army Group Centre had been given a bruising, Army Groups North and South were still relatively unaffected and that the Wehrmacht remained

A German soldier poses next to a knocked-out Soviet BT-5 light tank. The tank went into production in 1932 at a factory in Kharkov. It was armed with a 45mm tank gun and a coaxial machinegun as well as having 13mm of armour on the front plate. By World War II it had been reduced to the infantry support role. (Nik Cornish Library)

a strong and capable enemy, Zhukov argued for a single offensive directed at Army Group Centre, which was still off-balance and in disarray. Stalin's mind, however, was made up. The offensive was launched a few days later and, while it achieved some local successes, it was not strong enough to break through at any point. The Red Army was therefore left much weaker to face the German summer offensive and the shaky morale of the Wehrmacht was restored as it fought its first major defensive action.

At the end of March 1942, Stavka met to discuss strategy in relation to the coming summer campaign. Zhukov and the Deputy Chief of the General Staff, General Vasilevsky, advocated a defensive posture. Stalin, however, insisted on carrying out a series of localized offensives to effect the relief of the besieged cities of Leningrad in the north and Sebastopol in the Crimea, along with Marshal Timoshenko's proposal for a major attack aimed at recapturing Kharkov, out of the Barvenkovo Salient, which lay to the southeast of Kharkov. The city was the fourth biggest in the Soviet Union and a major road and rail junction and it would be the scene of several battles during the campaign on the Eastern Front. The offensive was to be conducted mainly by the Southwest Front (Timoshenko), with elements from the South Front (Malinovsky) providing support. The offensive would take the form of a pincer movement, with the Soviet 6th Army (Gorodnyanskov) forming the southern pincer, while a force under MajGen L.V. Bobkin moved towards Krasnograd to provide flank protection. In the area of Volchansk, the Soviet 28th Army (Ryabishev) with the adjacent 21st (Gordov) and 38th (Moskalenko) Armies would form the northern pincer. The two pincers would meet west of Kharkov and trap the German 6th Army. The 57th (Podlas) and 9th (Kharitonov) Armies from the Southern Front would protect the southern flank of the operation. While not hugely imaginative, its fatal flaw would be that it would commence just before the Germans were to begin Operation *Fridericus*, an attack aimed at eliminating the Barvenkovo salient.

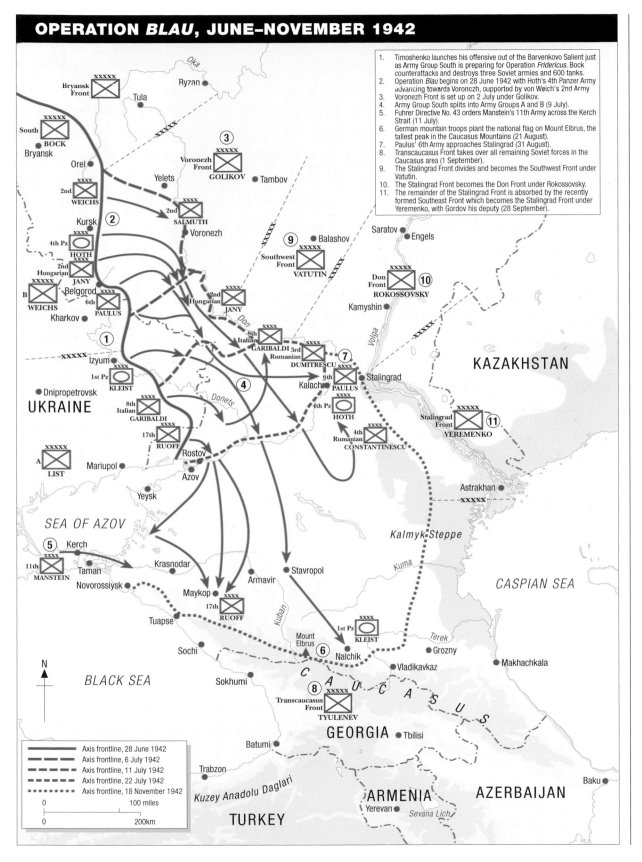

OPERATION *BLAU*, JUNE–NOVEMBER 1942

1. Timoshenko launches his offensive out of the Barvenkovo Salient just as Army Group South is preparing for Operation *Fridericus*. Bock counterattacks and destroys three Soviet armies and 600 tanks.
2. Operation *Blau* begins on 28 June 1942 with Hoth's 4th Panzer Army advancing towards Voronezh, supported by von Weich's 2nd Army.
3. Voronezh Front is set up on 2 July under Golikov.
4. Army Group South splits into Army Groups A and B (9 July).
5. Fuhrer Directive No. 43 orders Manstein's 11th Army across the Kerch Strait (11 July).
6. German mountain troops plant the national flag on Mount Elbrus, the tallest peak in the Caucasus Mountains (21 August).
7. Paulus' 6th Army approaches Stalingrad (31 August).
8. Transcaucasus Front takes over all remaining Soviet forces in the Caucasus area (1 September).
9. The Stalingrad Front divides and becomes the Southwest Front under Vatutin.
10. The Stalingrad Front becomes the Don Front under Rokossovsky.
11. The remainder of the Stalingrad Front is absorbed by the recently formed Southeast Front which becomes the Stalingrad Front under Yeremenko, with Gordov his deputy (28 September).

Axis frontline, 28 June 1942
Axis frontline, 6 July 1942
Axis frontline, 11 July 1942
Axis frontline, 22 July 1942
Axis frontline, 18 November 1942

0   100 miles
0   200km

THE CAMPAIGN

THE OPENING MOVES

Before Operation *Blau* could be put in effect, the Wehrmacht had two preliminary operations to carry out. The first was the reduction of the Soviet stronghold around the city of Sevastopol and the occupation of the Crimea, Operation *Störfang* (*Sturgeon Catch*), by von Manstein's 11th Army and the second, was the reduction of the Barvenkovo Salient just south of Kharkov (Operation *Fridericus*), both of which would provide jumping-off points for the Wehrmacht's offensive into the Caucasus. As GFM von Bock began to concentrate the 6th Army and 1st Panzer Army against the northern and southern faces of the salient, Marshal Timoshenko launched his offensive out of the salient, intending to retake Kharkov with a pincer movement by the 28th Army in the north and the 6th and 38th Armies in the south. These were supported by the 21st Army in the far north and the 9th and 57th Armies on the southern face of the salient. Although the northern pincer quickly ran into trouble, the southern pincer did very well, indeed rather too well. Timoshenko's main thrust seemed to be punching into thin air. The answer came on 17 May when probing patrols sent out to establish where the German forces were, came back with prisoners from the 1st Panzer

German walking wounded being treated prior to evacuation during Operation *Blau*, the German advance on the Caucasus. By the end of the campaign, Germany and its allies had suffered almost a million-and-a-half casualties and had had 50 divisions destroyed. (IWM, HU5145)

Army. Timoshenko realized that his armies were rolling straight into imminent danger and contacted Stavka in order to seek permission to slow the offensive down and reorganize his forces to meet the new threat from the south. Permission was refused – Kharkov had to be retaken.

The offensive, however, had indeed upset the German plan. It was obvious to von Bock that a two-pronged *Fridericus* was now impossible as the 6th Army was holding the northern pincer near Balakleya under immense Soviet pressure. Von Bock, therefore, decided on a modified *Fridericus* with an attack coming from the south consisting of the 1st Panzer Army and some infantry support from the 17th Army. The counter-attack began on 19 May and by 22 May 14th Panzer Division had reached the south bank of the Donets at Bayrak opposite the 44th Infantry Division. The pocket had closed and the majority of Timoshenko's assault force had been trapped inside. Some 29 Soviet divisions had been shattered, three armies (6th, 9th and 57th) had ceased to exist and four senior Soviet commanders, Kostenko, Bobkin, Podlas and Gorodnyanskov, lay dead. The Soviets suffered some 280,000 casualties and lost over 650 tanks and 5,000 guns. The Soviets had clearly underestimated their enemy in that Stalin and the Stavka believed they had come close to precipitating a German collapse on the Eastern Front with enemy forces, reserves and resources stretched to the limit and any major enemy action would be directed at Moscow. The Soviets learned some important lessons, however, including the wisdom of staying on the strategic defensive and of retreating before a major offensive rather than trying to hold ground.

Meanwhile, on 8 May von Manstein had begun the final operation to clear the Crimea, Operation *Stoerfang*. Von Manstein initially struck eastwards towards Kerch, defended by the Crimean Front. Poor defensive positioning and command and control meant that in less than a week, Soviet forces were streaming eastwards and the 11th Army was fighting in the outskirts of the city itself. Over the next few days, a beachhead evacuation was attempted but von Manstein battered the remnants of the Crimean Front with massed artillery and drove off the vessels of the Black Sea Fleet, with the Soviets losing over 176,000 men, 350 tanks and 3,500 guns (some 21 divisions).

Von Manstein then turned his attention to the Soviet fortress at Sevastopol. At dawn on 7 June, the 11th Army, supported by Rumanian forces, began their final attack which lasted for 27 days. Each Soviet position had to be ferociously bombarded and then closely assaulted in order to eliminate Soviet resistance with the giant emplacements such as Fort Stalin and Maksim Gorkii having to be bombarded by giant howitzers. As the Germans closed in, the supply line maintained by the Black Sea Fleet gave way, the city finally falling on 4 July. Tens of thousands of Soviet troops had been killed and another 95,000 taken prisoner but the Germans had suffered around 75,000 casualties themselves in close-quarter urban fighting that would prove to be a foretaste of what was to come at Stalingrad.

German tanks move out, with the Luftwaffe providing support in the background. The mobility of the Panzers allowed them to cover large distances very quickly, thereby encircling large pockets of enemy troops. Even though they had their own organic infantry (Panzer Grenadiers), they would still have to wait for the regular infantry to move up and reduce the enemy position. (IWM, HU5162)

BLAU BEGINS IN EARNEST

On 28 June, Army Group South launched Operation *Blau* (re-designated *Braunschweig* [*Brunswick*] after the Reichel incident) and their long drive towards the Caucasus. The Germans had rushed to start the operation before the discovery of the plans could be acted upon, but as it happened, Stalin still believed that the main German attack would be aimed at Moscow, and that any operation in the south was a diversion or a subsidiary operation at best. It would not be until early July that he would be forced to revise that assessment as it became increasingly clear that the operation in the south was one of significant magnitude. Von Bock began his attack by launching 4th Panzer Army (Hoth) towards Voronezh, a key town in lateral Soviet communications, with 2nd Army on its left flank. The Hungarian 2nd Army and 6th Army were to the south and the 6th Army started its advance two days later heading northeast towards the same target with the aim of encircling the Soviet 6th, 21st and 40th Armies between the three. Timoshenko refused to cooperate, given that his forces had received a severe blow in the Barvenkovo Salient and he was already numerically inferior. To stand and fight would have courted disaster but, on the other hand, Voronezh had to be held as its fall would imperil Soviet communications, allow the Germans to take the Bryansk Front in the rear and then potentially advance on Moscow. Stavka was not to know that Moscow was not on the German agenda and so, as the German forces were moving into position, Stavka rushed further reserves into the area and set up a new headquarters at Voronezh under Golikov and Vasilevsky. These forces moved into the area just after the Germans had seized a bridgehead on the Don and were on the outskirts of the city. Army Group South diverted the XXIV Panzer Corps and three infantry divisions to deal with this threat. This created a dilemma within the German High Command who were surprised by the stubbornness with which the Soviets defended Voronezh. The Soviets did so as they feared it was the first move in a strike on Moscow but in German plans the capture of Voronezh was secondary to the encirclement of Timoshenko's forces as there was in fact no intention to strike north. While the 4th Panzer Army battled to take the city, the Southwest Front gradually withdrew and Soviet

German mountain troops advancing into the Caucasus with a camel. The soldiers still have their greatcoats on, indicating the low temperature. It is unclear if they have actively acquired the camel or have just come across it while travelling. (Nik Cornish Library)

German troops moving into the outskirts of Stalingrad. For the German infantry, combat within this large built-up area, often going on 24 hours a day, would prove to be a very different experience to that of the manoeuvre warfare used in blitzkrieg. (IWM, HU5157)

reserves continued to arrive. There were so many, in fact, that a new formation, the Voronezh Front, was set up making it dangerous for the 4th Panzer Army to withdraw, lest Soviet forces should be given the opportunity to counter-attack. The army would not free itself until 13 July. Hitler finally lost patience and dismissed von Bock, implementing the next phase of the operation which saw Army Group South split into Army Groups A and B, the former to handle the drive to the Caucasus and the latter to handle the drive on the Volga. Hitler then moved his headquarters from Rastenburg to Vinnitsa in the Ukraine and issued a radical revision to the operational schedule on 23 July 1942, in the form of Fuhrer Directive No. 45.

At this point in the campaign, the Germans seemed to have repeated the early successes of the previous summer. Another month would see German forces on the Volga and on the outskirts of Stalingrad. Farther south they were in the foothills of the Caucasus, had occupied Maykop and were poised to seize Grozny. They would then advance on Baku and occupy the entire east coast of the Black Sea. On 21 August 1942, the German flag was raised on Mount Elbrus, the highest peak in the Caucasus Mountains. This was the point at which the Germans had most deeply penetrated the Soviet Union, bringing almost half of its population and resources under their control. During July and August, the Germans captured around 625,000 Soviet prisoners, captured or destroyed over 7,000 tanks, 6,000 artillery pieces and 400 aircraft to add to those already captured during May and June. These losses were high, but were not on the scale of 1941 and the Germans suffered significant casualties as well – almost 200,000 in August alone. The reason was simple: the Soviets, after Stavka had issued a general retreat order on 6 July 1942, had chosen to withdraw rather than to stand and fight. This meant that the Germans, while occupying large swathes of territory, were not achieving their other goal of destroying enemy forces in sufficient numbers to cause the Red Army to crumble. This was the problem with operations based on deep penetration and large-scale envelopment. Their success depended on the enemy preferring (or having) to stand and fight rather than trying to evade encirclement and surrender territory. However, from the German point of view, these sweeping gains were confirmation that the Red Army was weak and in full retreat and its impact upon Hitler showed itself in the strategic re-orientation that started in early July and was finally encapsulated in Directive No. 45.

The original conception of *Blau* was that its objectives would be achieved on a phased basis, that Army Group South would destroy the Soviet forces between Yelets and Rostov, occupy the Don Basin, advance to and then secure the Volga and then advance south to the Causasus. On 9 July Army Group South was prematurely split into Army Groups A and B and, a few days later, von Bock who was to have commanded Army Group A, was dismissed and replaced by GFM Wilhelm List. Von Bock had wanted to deal with Vatutin's Voronezh Front before moving southeast and had proposed to use 2nd Army (von Weichs) and elements of 6th Army (Paulus) to do so. This, of course, made operational sense, especially since von Bock had had personal experience in the previous summer of the delays and frustrations inherent in leaving large formations of Soviet troops intact on a flank. Had von Bock been allowed to do what he wanted the course of the entire campaign in the south may well have been different, as might the course of the war. In addition, Fuhrer Directive No. 43 ordered von Manstein and the majority of the 11th Army northwards where its experience in siege operations would be of benefit to Army Group North which was still besieging Leningrad. The 4th Panzer Army was directed to join Army Group A and assist 1st Panzer Army's attack towards Rostov. Directive No. 45 now tasked Army Group A with destroying Soviet forces in front of Rostov, moving south and occupying the entire eastern coast of the Black Sea and taking control of the oil-producing area around Maykop, Grozny and Baku in an operation codenamed *Edelweiss*. Army Group B, now reduced to 2nd Army, 6th Army and the Axis satellite armies, would advance on Stalingrad, take it and occupy the narrow land corridor between the Don and Volga rivers. As it turned out, the re-direction of 4th Panzer Army proved to be of little benefit to Army Group A as Kleist's forces didn't need any help as the South Front was already withdrawing over the river.

The Red Army, however, also had its problems. Public morale had been badly affected by the reverses during May, June and July and was highly critical of the lack of leadership apparent in the south and contrasted this with the stout defenders of both Leningrad and Moscow. This caused long-lasting tensions between the commanders on the spot and those sent down from Stavka. Had Timoshenko been allowed to halt his May offensive and withdraw his forces when he first asked permission, the Southwest Front would have been in a much better position to withstand the German attack. The real culprits of the piece were Stalin and Stavka, something the southern commanders knew but the majority of the armed forces and the public did not. All they could see was that the precious industrial capacity, carefully built up during years of sacrifice in the recent past was being handed over to the German invader. Stavka was, however, able to start moving reserves into the area but, as they had been kept in the centre to protect Moscow, they did not start moving until early July and were kept behind the Don bend and Timoshenko's retreating forces. To have committed them piecemeal would have helped slow the German advance but run the risk of their being destroyed as they were committed. Having them shielded behind the front line and a major geographical obstacle meant they went relatively undetected by the Germans. This confirmed the German belief that the Soviets had no operational reserves to speak of and their subsequent actions based on this belief were to prove catastrophic. Directive No. 45 meant that *Blau* would now be eclipsed (at least partially) by *Edelweiss* and the two strategic objectives that were once to be achieved in sequence would now be pursued simultaneously. The Germans were not strong enough to achieve both at the same time. It is also doubtful if they could have achieved their objectives in the Caucasus (at least quickly), short of a complete Soviet collapse, as distance, logistics and terrain were against them. They may, however, have taken Stalingrad quickly had they concentrated on taking that before moving on to the Caucasus. As it was, the 6th Army, especially with 4th Panzer Army having been diverted south, was neither strong enough nor quick enough to reach the city before the Soviets had time to build up their defences and start moving in reinforcements.

Rostov was recaptured on 24 July 1942, having been in German hands in November 1941. On 1 August, 4th Panzer Army, having just started to get their vehicles across the Don, were reassigned back to Army Group B and tasked with taking Stalingrad from the south, with a single division moving south to maintain contact with 1st Panzer Army. Too much time had been wasted and too much momentum lost for 4th Panzer Army to make a difference to 6th Army's progress but its redeployment signified that Stalingrad had begun to capture the German imagination. Stalingrad was the pivot on which the whole defence line for continuing *Edelweiss* hinged – to commit two armies to its capture would mean there would be no going back. Regardless of the arguments for or against capturing the city as opposed to just bringing it under fire and controlling the Volga, politically and psychologically its capture became vital and a failure to achieve this would have serious consequences for both the Axis and the Allies in terms of alliance politics and morale. This Hitler understood better than his generals. Meanwhile, by early July, the Soviets had begun to realize the seriousness of the German offensive and the growing importance of defending Stalingrad. On 12 July, Stalin ordered the creation of the Stalingrad Front, a force of some 38 divisions (of which half were under-strength) consisting of three reserve armies. This was initially commanded by Timoshenko but command quickly passed to Gordov and finally to Yeremenko.

On 19 July, Stalingrad itself was put on an immediate war footing. On 28 July, Stalin issued Order No. 227, the famous 'Not One Step Back' order. This was read to the armed forces and officers were required to

German soldiers at rest near a Panzer IV. The Panzer IV was the only German tank to be in series production all the way through the war, with over 9,000 being made, and was continuously upgraded to keep abreast of battlefield developments. (IWM, HU5148)

German infantry advancing into Stalingrad, alongside a Stug III. Tanks and assault guns would be vulnerable targets if entering an urban area unaccompanied but would make a useful mobile artillery piece if fighting alongside infantry as part of a combined arms team. (IWM, HU5150)

sign a declaration that they had read it. It was a declaration setting out the dire situation facing the USSR and calling on the armed forces to do their patriotic duty and defend the Motherland. It was a call for a controlled, disciplined retreat and for a last defence centred on Stalingrad. Its effects on the armed forces seem to have been mixed but in general it was received with enthusiasm and many found it inspiring. It was similar in tone to Churchill's 'Blood, Toil, Tears and Sweat' speech in May 1940 when Britain was under threat. This went hand-in-hand with intense 'hate' propaganda aimed at demonizing the opposition and bolstering the population's will to resist. This had been going on since the early days of the invasion and continued into the current campaign as the Nazi philosophy regarding the *Untermensch* (subhuman) reached its peak in the east with every report, photograph and newspaper article exhorting the racial inferiority of the enemy.

The final strand of Soviet mobilization was the increasing nationalisation and professionalization of the armed forces. After *Barbarossa*, Stalin moved to exert greater party control over the armed forces but, as the battle for Stalingrad took shape, party–army relations took a different turn and the official press was filled with articles exhorting the importance of professionalism, leadership ability and technical skill rather than ideological dogma. Officers suddenly assumed a huge importance in the defence of the Motherland and special decorations were introduced just for officers, including the orders of Kutuzov, Nevsky and Suvorov. Later, distinctive new uniforms were introduced for officers that included epaulettes and gold braid. Next in this process was the abolition of the institution of the commissars, which had been a system of dual decision-making in the armed forces whereby the commissars exercised both political and military control over command decisions. Henceforth, officers would take command decisions alone, and the commissars would advise on military matters and concentrate on political affairs among the troops. This professionalization of relations extended to the strategic level with General Alexander M. Vasilevsky being appointed Chief of the

Soviet troops fighting in a ruined factory. Often, Soviet troops would take up positions virtually next to the enemy, or keep them engaged, to ensure that the Germans could not easily use their advantage in air and artillery support for fear of hitting their own troops. (IWM, HU3551)

General Staff on 26 June and Zhukov, the saviour of Leningrad and Moscow, being appointed Deputy Supreme Commander of the Armed Forces on 26 August. Stalin was more and more relying on their judgement in military affairs and was increasingly ready to defer to that judgement.

The contrast with the German war effort could not have been greater. Hitler increasingly subordinated and dominated his senior commanders and held them in ever-greater contempt. Not only had von Bock been dismissed but in September, as the Caucasus campaign and the battle for Stalingrad were at their height, he dismissed first von List, the commander of Army Group A, for not making satisfactory progress in taking the Caucasus (despite clearly not having the forces to do so, especially after the reallocation of 4th Panzer Army back to Army Group B) and then Halder, who as time progressed had come to fear that Directive No. 45 and the attempt to capture Stalingrad and the Caucasus simultaneously would mean German defeat. After deliberately provoking Hitler, he was dismissed as the Chief of Staff for OKH and replaced by General Kurt Zeitzler. It is clear that the single most identifiable cause of the German defeat at Stalingrad was Hitler's impact on the command process, his decision to split the German effort on two divergent objectives and his willingness to continue to fight for the city even though it was becoming increasingly clear that the Soviets were drawing the Germans into a costly war of attrition.

THE GERMANS ADVANCE ON STALINGRAD

By 22 July, Army Group B had reached positions close to the Don river that it hoped would provide jumping-off points for the final advance on Stalingrad, while Army Group A had reached the lower Don river and was ready to embark upon *Edelweiss*. Army Group B was to be divided into three sub-groups and 6th Army. The northern group of two Panzer, two motorized and four infantry divisions, was to attack on 23 July from the Golovsky–Perelazovsky area with a view to capturing the large bridge over the Don river at Kalach behind the Soviet forces deployed west of the river. The central group, of one Panzer and two infantry divisions was to attack from the Oblivskaya–Verkhne–Aksenovsky area, also heading for Kalach, and, with the northern group, form a blocking force to the rear of the Soviet forces against which 6th Army would advance east and crush them, leaving the road to the Volga open. This was an opportunity to be exploited by the southern force, of one Panzer, one motorized and four infantry divisions that were to cross the Don river near Tsimlyanskaya on 21 July, forming a bridgehead from which to advance on the city from the south. For this mission, Army Group B commander, GenObst von Weichs, had a force of about 30 divisions, although only just over half were German, with air support provided by over 1,200 aircraft. They outnumbered the Soviet forces in the Don bend about two-to-one in troops, although a more serious disparity existed in heavy weapons due to the losses the Southwest Front incurred around Kharkov.

On 23 July, five German divisions attacked the right wing of 62nd Army while the 64th Army was also engaged on the Tsimla river. After three days of fighting, XIV Panzer Corps broke through the Soviet lines and advanced to the Don river, outflanking 62nd Army to the north. The 1st Tank Army, deployed in reserve, tried to cut the German forces off by attacking northwards across its line of advance while 4th Tank Army tried to head off the German attack from the north. Unfortunately neither army had been in existence for very long and contained a heterogeneous mix of tanks and infantry that had had little time to train with one another so neither attack proved successful. Meanwhile, XXIV Panzer Corps continued to drive a wedge between 62nd and 64th Armies as it headed towards Kalach from the southwest. Gordov was ordered to strengthen his southern defences and deployed 57th Army to stop further German penetration, as well as being given 51st Army to command. This meant that Stalingrad Front's line stretched for over 400 miles and so Stavka decided to form a new front to take over the southern part of the line, the Southeast Front. The 4th Panzer Army had managed to cross the Don and Hoth now attacked the over-extended 51st Army on 31 July in an effort to reach Tsimlyanskaya. The German attack broke through easily and, while the Soviets tried to withdraw towards the Tikhoretsk–Krasnoarmeysk railway, 4th Panzer Army headed northeast, reaching Kotelnikovo by 2 August. Farther north, 62nd Army had lost most of its infantry in the German envelopment and, while it would recover many of them in small groups, they had lost most of their heavy equipment, although it did gain the remnants of 1st Tank Army which had been disbanded. In their great haste to advance on the city, though, the Germans left portions of the south bank of the Don in the possession of the 1st

German infantry in a ruined building on the outskirts of Stalingrad, during the early fighting for the city. They seem to be led by the NCO on the right, who is armed with an MP40 sub-machinegun and who looks as if he is considering the best way to continue the advance. (IWM, HU5131)

Guards and 21st Armies and, with the 3rd Rumanian Army standing resolutely on the defensive, this would prove to be a costly oversight later in the battle.

The Soviet resistance encountered in the Don bend convinced Paulus that 6th Army was not strong enough to force a crossing of the river by itself, so a lull followed as he waited for Hoth's Panzers to fight their way north. Gradually, the balance in numbers shifted against the Soviets as the 64th Army, which had played an important role in stiffening the 62nd Army's resistance, had to extend its left flank eastwards to cover 4th Panzer Army's approach. On 5 August, Yeremenko arrived at the new Tsaritsyn bunker and was scheduled to take over command of the new Southeast Front four days later but had little time to organize his command. Hoth, approaching from the south, attacked the 64th Army, just as 6th Army had drawn itself up into position facing due east, and had von Richthofen's VIII Fliegerkorps, newly installed at the Morozovsk airfield complex, in support. Eventually, Hoth caved in the left flank of 64th Army and found himself within 19 miles of the city. His penetration was only halted after Yeremenko sent down a mixed force of tanks, infantry and artillery which stopped Hoth at Abganerovo. While the German advance had been temporarily stopped, the situation was still dire. The natural line of advance was along the very division of responsibility between the Stalingrad and Southeast fronts, with all the difficulties that would entail in coordinating the actions of two commands, with commanders of equal status, especially in the movement and allocation of reserves. Yeremenko reported the difficulty to Stavka, which moved surprisingly quickly and designated him as the overall commander of both fronts with Gordov as his deputy for the Stalingrad Front and Golikov (formerly of the Bryansk Front) the deputy for the Southeast Front.

There was little respite to be had. Conscious that Hitler had given 25 August as the deadline for the control of the city, Paulus (as the senior commander) gave orders that the attack to capture Stalingrad would begin on 23 August. Late on 22 August, Wietersheim's XIV Panzer Corps managed to open a narrow breach in the Soviet defences near Vertyachi and the next day managed to fight its way across into the northern suburbs of the city, even reaching the Volga that evening. It seemed to Paulus and von Weichs that Stalingrad was within their grasp.

German pioneers working to convert the wide Russian-gauge railway to the narrower European standard. As the Wehrmacht advanced, this sort of work would be vital as the road system in southern Russia was primitive at best and so the railway would be vital in keeping the forces supplied. (Nik Cornish Library)

FOOTHILLS OF THE CAUCASUS, 13 AUGUST 1942.
(Pages 46–47)

Fuhrer Directive 41 laid out the basis for Operation Blau, the German summer offensive for 1942 on the Eastern Front and set its main objective as the oilfields in the southern Caucasus, around Maykop, Grozny and Baku. Army Group South would undertake the offensive and this was, in the original plans, to be achieved in a phased basis. First, Army Group South would destroy the Soviet forces south of the Don River and then advance along and secure the river, eventually bringing Stalingrad under fire and cutting the Volga River, a major artery for oil supplies heading north. The army group would then split into two, Army Groups A and B, with B continuing to hold the river line and A advancing southwards into the Caucasus and capturing the oilfields. With the opening phases of the operation netting fewer than expected Soviet prisoners, and German forces advancing with relative ease, Hitler assumed that the Soviet forces in the south were weaker than anticipated and prematurely split Army Group South under Fuhrer Directive No. 45. Army Groups A and B would have to pursue two major operational objectives simultaneously (which would come to include taking and holding Stalingrad) instead of sequentially. While Army Group B under von Weichs headed for Stalingrad, Army Group A under List, consisting of the 17th and 1st Panzer Armies, along with elements of the 11th Army, advanced south. Where the 17th Army under Ruoff made only steady progress, the 1st Panzer Army under von Kleist roamed at will, as the Transcaucasus Front under Tyulenev had few heavy weapons with which to oppose him and the Germans' supply problems were eased (temporarily) by the seizure of the Crimea. As the 1st Panzer Army ground on towards Grozny, the XXXXIV Corps on its right (with two German and one Rumanian mountain divisions) were making steady progress into the Caucasus Mountains, heading for the Klukhorskiy Pass. The German troops lacked the heavy weapons with which to blast their way through and struggled against the hardening resistance as shown here: the vanguard (1) of a column of Gebirgsjäger has just been ambushed by Soviet troops (2) entrenched on the hillside. These are hasty positions with only the minimum of care taken over their concealment with a few rocks and boulders used to camouflage the trenches. The Soviets troops have opened fire before the Germans have reached the closest possible point for fear that they might have been spotted and the alarm raised before achieving surprise. This has meant that while the longer ranged weapons, such as the Moisin-Nagant rifles (3), DP-28 light machinegun (4) and PTRD antitank rifle (5) have been able to engage effectively, the PPSh-41 (6) and PPS-42 (7) submachineguns are at a disadvantage due to the range. While the initial attack has achieved surprise, causing several casualties, most of the German troops are in the process of taking cover and are starting to return fire. The rest of the column (8) has seen the ambush take place and is quickly deploying to set up a mountain howitzer, carried on some pack animals and to out-flank the attackers.

With Wietersheim encamped on the Volga and the bridge at Rynok within mortar range, it seemed that the problem of supplying, let alone reinforcing the garrison, would be almost impossible to overcome. Seydlitz's LI Corps followed Wieterscheim into the breach and it looked as if the 62nd Army would be rolled up. The Germans, however, underestimated the Soviet determination to fight in front of and, if necessary, in Stalingrad. While Wieterscheim managed to keep his corridor open, he could not expand it and 62nd Army managed to withdraw along the Karpova and the railway line that ran parallel. By sheer force the 4th Panzer Army moved 64th Army back but it was obvious that there would be no breakthrough.

Meanwhile, Army Group A had crossed the Don river and started advancing on the Caucasus Mountains, taking Proletarskaya on 29 July, Salsk on 31 July and Stavropol on 5 August. Kleist's 1st Panzer Army was roaming at will in the foothills of the Caucasus, having had its supply problems eased considerably with the clearing of the Crimea by von Manstein's 11th Army and both his and Ruoff's supply trains were re-routed across the Kerch Peninsula into the Kuban. Maykop fell on 9 August and, shortly afterwards, Pyatigorsk. Soviet resistance in the Caucasus was badly hindered by a lack of heavy weapons and tanks and, wherever Kleist deployed his tanks, the Soviet infantry and cavalry were obliged to retreat. But even now, the growing demands of the fighting around Stalingrad were beginning to starve him of supplies and replacements. Having made a detour through Rostov, many of his vehicles were becoming increasingly unreliable as many had only been patched up after the rigours of *Barbarossa* and were in need of a major overhaul. In addition to this, in obeying the vaguely worded instructions in Directive No. 45, Kleist was pursuing several important objectives at once, including trying to break through to the Caspian and either to occupy or destroy the oil complex at Baku, capture Tiflis, the capital of the Caucasus and support the remainder of List's Army Group A in its drive into the Caucasus and down the eastern Black Sea coast to isolate the Black Sea fleet. As it was, all eyes were on Stalingrad.

Paulus renewed his attack on 24 and 25 August but the attack met a Soviet defence that was going to fight for every yard of ground. This constant and unyielding willingness to defend every square foot of the city as well as the sudden loss of a prize that had seemed to be within easy reach led the Germans to apply more and more force at the tip of an increasingly vulnerable front as the battle drew in the surrounding German forces, leaving little in the way of reserves to back up the Axis divisions on either flank.

A German PAK 36 3.7cm anti-tank gun. The standard German anti-tank gun at the outbreak of war, it was produced by Rheinmetall. While effective against lightly armoured targets, crews would have to wait until point-blank range before taking on heavier tanks. The use of tungsten-cored and shaped charge ammunition improved effectiveness. (IWM, HU5166)

Elements of the 21st Army attacked German positions near Serafimovich and Kletskaya but were not strong enough to penetrate, neither were counter-attacks in the vicinity of Samofalovka, but the 1st Guards Army attack near Novo-Grigoryevskaya extended its bridgehead as did the 63rd Army's. To the south, 4th Panzer Army had been attempting to break through to Stalingrad but had failed to make any progress against a series of well-defended Soviet strongpoints south of the city. Tanks and motorized infantry were quietly moved around to the southwestern part of the front, reorganized near Abganerovo and launched on 29 August against the 126th Rifle Division of 64th Army. Hoth wanted to drive a wedge into the centre of the 64th Army and then turn right into the rear of the difficult Soviet strongpoints to capture the bank of the Volga and high ground south of the city and to cut off the left wing of the 64th Army. The attack, supported by the Luftwaffe, succeeded beyond expectations and Hoth's forces found themselves in the rear areas of both the 64th and 62nd Armies. A bigger prize was now suddenly possible: if 4th Panzer Army continued north instead of wheeling right the right flank of 64th Army and perhaps the whole of 62nd Army might be trapped if 6th Army moved south to meet it. Weichs reacted quickly and twice ordered 6th Army to move south to meet 4th Panzer Army. Paulus, however, did not move – the Soviet counter-attacks had persuaded both Wiedersheim and himself that the northern sector was very precarious and that if he sent his mobile forces south the northern sector might collapse. It wasn't until 2 September that the pressure on Paulus relaxed and he immediately sent his tanks and motorized infantry south to make contact with Hoth. At the same time Seydlitz's infantry made contact with the forward elements of 4th Panzer Army. The Soviets, however, had gone. Yeremenko, not realizing that Hoth had originally been after the left wing of the 64th Army, had assumed that the Germans were after the right wing of 64th and the whole of 62nd and started to withdraw his forces. He effectively abandoned the outer defences of Stalingrad just as the Germans had realized the opportunity that was before them. In one sense, the German moves had paid

Soviet infantry in action, supported in the foreground by a soldier carrying an ROKS-2 flame-thrower. These were originally issued to individual infantry units but were gradually pulled back and issued to specialist troops as a divisional asset. (Central Museum of the Armed Forces, Moscow)

dividends as they could now attack directly into the city from all directions without having to break through an outer defence line, while on the other hand, Yeremenko's counter-attacks had mostly failed. They had, however, pinned Paulus for a few vital days, which meant that the 6th Army delayed in joining up with 4th Panzer Army, allowing Yeremenko's forces to escape. The Germans could now directly interdict the river lifeline across which supplies and reinforcements would have to move, mainly at night, and the battle for the city itself was about to begin.

THE ASSAULT BEGINS

As the 6th Army and 4th Panzer Army approached Stalingrad it looked as if the Germans would be able to take the city after a short fight. As at Moscow, however, the terrain to the west of Stalingrad was difficult to manoeuvre across. The urban character of the city, with its enormous factories and sprawling settlements would prove a hindrance to the effective coordination of armour, artillery, air power and infantry that lay at the heart of the highly effective blitzkrieg tactics employed by the Wehrmacht. The city itself was a peculiar shape in that it was long and narrow (25 miles long and five miles in depth) and stretched along the western bank of the Volga, which was one mile wide at this point. The Germans, therefore, could not use their normal tactics of envelopment and had to conduct a frontal assault on the city. The northern end of the city was dominated by the great factories: the Dzerzhinsky Tractor Factory, the Barrikady Ordnance Factory which had the Silikat Factory in front of it and the Krasny Oktyabr Steel Plant, to the south of which lay the Lazur Chemical Plant. This formed a single interconnected fortified position that would see intense fighting over the coming months. The southern end of the city was divided from the rest by the Tsaritsa river flowing directly into the Volga from just south of the Stalingrad No. 1 Railway Station. To the south of the river lay the suburbs of Minina and Yelshanka where Shumilov's 64th Army lay, securing the flank of the 62nd Army under Gen Lopatin. He was replaced on 12 September by Vasily Chuikov. Chuikov had briefly commanded the 64th Army and an *ad hoc* force that had stopped the 4th Panzer Army south of Stalingrad. He had studied German tactical methods, for which he held a great deal of respect. He had, however, discerned a possible weakness in the German armour which would prove useful in the fighting to come. The German ability to integrate all the different elements of the modern battlefield into a cohesive whole and wield it effectively had been astonishing. However, the armour rarely moved before the air power attacked and the infantry followed the armour. In the countryside of Western Europe and on the steppes of the USSR this had been the secret of the German success but such methods would be far more difficult to implement within an urban environment. Chuikov knew he could not entirely remove the Luftwaffe (for it had mastery of the skies above Stalingrad), but he wanted to find some way of blunting its impact. His solution would be to deploy his men as close as possible, sometimes within hand-grenade range, to German positions. This would mean the Luftwaffe would not be able to attack without hitting their own troops. The German Panzers and infantry would

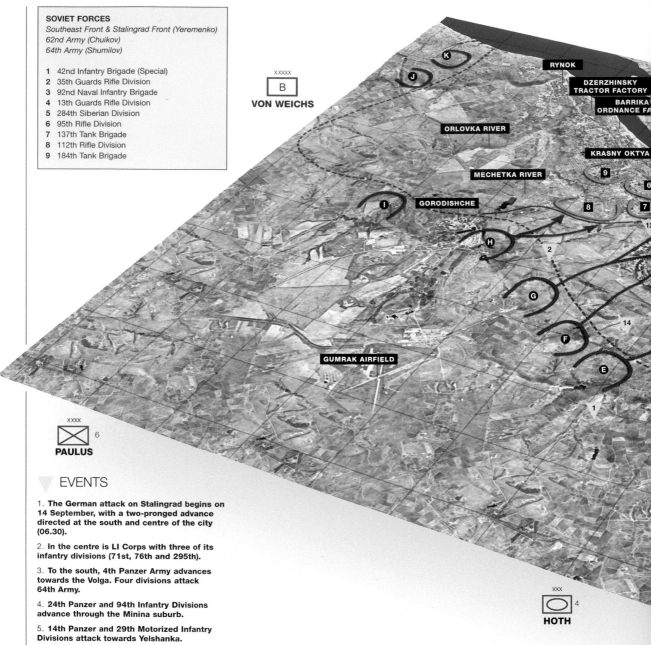

SOVIET FORCES
Southeast Front & Stalingrad Front (Yeremenko)
62nd Army (Chuikov)
64th Army (Shumilov)

1. 42nd Infantry Brigade (Special)
2. 35th Guards Rifle Division
3. 92nd Naval Infantry Brigade
4. 13th Guards Rifle Division
5. 284th Siberian Division
6. 95th Rifle Division
7. 137th Tank Brigade
8. 112th Rifle Division
9. 184th Tank Brigade

xxxxx
B
VON WEICHS

RYNOK
DZERZHINSKY TRACTOR FACTORY
BARRIKA ORDNANCE FA
KRASNY OKTYA

ORLOVKA RIVER

MECHETKA RIVER

K
J
I
H
G
F
E

9
8
7
6

2

14

1

GORODISHCHE

GUMRAK AIRFIELD

xxxx
6
PAULUS

xxx
4
HOTH

▼ EVENTS

1. **The German attack on Stalingrad begins on 14 September, with a two-pronged advance directed at the south and centre of the city (06.30).**

2. **In the centre is LI Corps with three of its infantry divisions (71st, 76th and 295th).**

3. **To the south, 4th Panzer Army advances towards the Volga. Four divisions attack 64th Army.**

4. **24th Panzer and 94th Infantry Divisions advance through the Minina suburb.**

5. **14th Panzer and 29th Motorized Infantry Divisions attack towards Yelshanka.**

6. **Chuikov is forced to evacuate his command post on Mamayev Kurgan (14.00).**

7. **13th Guards Rifle Division lands and secures the area around the landing stages (19.00).**

8. **Chuikov launches a counterattack against Mamayev Kurgan with elements of the 13th Guards and 112th Rifle Divisions (16 September).**

9. **The 92nd Naval Infantry and 137th Tank Brigades are transferred across the Volga (17 September).**

10. **Elements of the 14th Panzer, 24th Panzer and 94th Infantry Divisions engage in a prolonged struggle for the Grain Elevator with a small number of troops from the 92nd Naval Infantry Brigade and 35th Guards Rifle Division (18-22 September).**

11. **After several days of heavy fighting, the German 76th Infantry Division secures the Stalingrad No. 1 Station (19 September).**

12. **The 284th Siberian Division moves across the river to support the 13th Guards and 112th Rifle Divisions and to stop the German 71st Infantry Division (23 September).**

13. **Chuikov's left flank crumbles as the German onslaught succeeds in reaching the Volga after taking the Stalingrad No. 1 Station and Grain Elevator, while the shattered remnants of the 35th Guards Rifle Division, 92nd Naval Infantry and 42nd Infantry Brigades withdraw across the river (25-26 September).**

14. **Paulus transfers units northwards after declaring the southern part of the city secure, in preparation for the second assault (26 September).**

KEY

German positions 14 September

Russian positions 14 September

Front line 14 September

Front line 26 September

GERMAN ASSAULT ON STALINGRAD: 14–26 SEPTEMBER 1942

The first German assault on the south and centre of Stalingrad gets underway on 14 September and, despite heavy fighting, meets its objectives. There are already indications, however, that this will not be a walkover.

xxxx
62
CHUIKOV

xxxxx
Southeast Front
YEREMENKO

xxxxx
Stalingrad Front
YEREMENKO

Note: Gridlines are shown at intervals of 3km/1.86miles

N

KRASNAYA SLOBADA

MAMAYEV KURGAN

6
9 4 7
9
13
10
3
YELSHANKA
4
MININA
2 1
KUPOROSNOYE

D C 3
5
B
RIVER VOLGA

A

xxxx
64
SHUMILOV

GERMAN FORCES
Army Group B (von Weichs)
6th Army (Paulus)
4th Panzer Army (Hoth)

A 29th Motorised Infantry Division
B 14th Panzer Division
C 94th Infantry Division
D 24th Panzer Division
E 76th Infantry Division
F 71st Infantry Division
G 295th Infantry Division
H 100th Jäger Division
I 389th Infantry Division
J 60th Motorised Infantry Division
K 16th Panzer Division

have to battle their way forward at close quarters in an urban setting – their least favoured tactical environment. Even though 62nd Army would be outnumbered and outgunned, it would still stand some chance of success. As he explained later, Chuikov wanted every German soldier in Stalingrad to be 'made to feel he lives under the muzzle of a Russian gun ... It occurred to us, therefore, that we should reduce the no-man's-land as much as possible close enough to the throw of a grenade ...'

The fighting and manoeuvring around the perimeter of Stalingrad had meant that both 6th Army and 4th Panzer Army had become strung out and so it took time for them to concentrate again and prepare for an all-out assault on the city. On the eve of the assault, the Germans faced a total of nine Soviet armies along a 400-mile front under the command of the Stalingrad and Southeast Fronts. The Southeast Front contained the 62nd, 64th, 57th and 51st Armies. Chuikov's 62nd Army was deployed in the city, with 54,000 troops, 900 artillery pieces and 100 tanks. The German 6th Army contained 15 divisions. To the northwest sat XI Corps with four divisions keeping an eye on the Soviet 21st Army and 4th Tank Army across the Don. To their right and immediately north of the city lay VIII Corps with two divisions and the XIV Panzer Corps now commanded by GenLt Hans Hube. To the west of the city was the LI Corps who were preparing to storm it with five divisions and supported on its left flank by 60th Motorized Infantry Division from XIV Panzer Corps. The 4th Panzer Army was deployed to the south of the Tsaritsa, with four divisions (94th Infantry, 29th Motorized, 14th and 24th Panzer) facing the left flank of the 62nd Army and the remaining two divisions (297th and 371st Infantry) deployed on the far right flank facing 64th Army. The basic Soviet units of army, corps, division and brigade were generally smaller than their German equivalents. The 6th Army was in fact the size of a Soviet front, at around 300,000 strong; a Soviet army was similar in size to a German corps at around 60–70,000 strong and a full-strength Panzer division, weighing in at around 18,000 was larger than a Soviet tank or mechanised corps at that time. The tank corps consisted of three tank brigades of around 60 tanks each,

German troops advancing through the Barrikady (Barricade) Ordnance Works during the third phase of the battle in October 1942. The 6th Army managed to advance to the Volga River in several places, splitting Chuikov's forces into three small groups. (IWM, HU5134)

a mechanized brigade, a reconnaissance battalion, mortar battalion and artillery battalion for a total strength of 7,800 troops, which was about the same as a Panzer regiment. A mechanized corps consisted of three mechanized brigades, each with a tank regiment plus one or two tank brigades as well as the usual supporting arms and totalled about 13,559 troops. The final formation, a Soviet infantry division, totalled about 10,500 troops, around two thirds the size of its German counterpart.

The first German assault on the city began at 06.30hrs on 14 September with the LI Corps attacking directly towards the city centre in a two-pronged assault. This caught Chuikov off guard as he was planning a series of small-scale counter-attacks. The LI Corps was led by the 71st, 76th and 295th Infantry Divisions while, south of the Tsaritsa, 4th Panzer Army attacked 64th Army with the 24th Panzer and 94th Infantry Divisions moving through the Minina suburbs and the 14th Panzer and 29th Motorized Division heading for the Volga through the Yelshanka area. This two-pronged assault revealed that the Germans were even now trying to use encirclement tactics with 4th Panzer, aiming to drive north upon reaching the Volga. LI Corps, meanwhile, after occupying central Stalingrad and Mamayev Kurgan, would head south and the two would meet at the central landing stage to isolate 62nd Army from its source of supply. The Germans managed to take Mamayev Kurgan and the Stalingrad-1 Railway Station and were approaching the landing stage. Chuikov pleaded with Yeremenko for reinforcements. The 13th Guards Division was sent over and, after bitter fighting, secured the landing stage. The division was attacked by elements of the German 71st and 295th Infantry Divisions and, after a bloody battle lasting several days during which the railway station changed hands some 19 times, the German 76th Infantry Division was committed and finally captured the station. The 13th Guards had bought time for Chuikov to rearrange his defences and for further reinforcements to cross the river, although it paid for its success with 75 per cent casualties.

The fighting for Mamayev Kurgan was equally intense. The German 295th Infantry Division made an all-out attack early on, forcing Chuikov to abandon his command post, and eventually occupied the hill. This was an important tactical position as it would provide the Germans with a clear view of both flanks of 62nd Army, the movement of supplies and reinforcements from the rear and would allow them to bring the Volga crossings under sustained and accurate artillery fire. Chuikov ordered two infantry regiments to attack and secure the hill on 17 September. After a short barrage, the Soviets attacked and, despite heavy casualties, reached the summit but could not secure the hill. The fighting continued for several days with repeated attacks by the Luftwaffe. However, the Soviets counter-attacked north of Stalingrad with 1st Guards, 24th and 66th Armies against the German VIII and XIV Panzer Corps, drawing off Luftwaffe support. The attack failed due to heavy German opposition and poor coordination but it allowed Chuikov to bring across two reinforcing brigades – 92nd Naval Infantry and 137th Tank. Chuikov attacked Mamayev Kurgan again, with no result. The 13th Guards lost its grip on Stalingrad-1 Railway Station as the German 71st Infantry Division renewed its assault with the aim of reaching the Volga and rolling up the 13th Guards' left flank, isolating 62nd Army and meeting up with the 76th and 295th Infantry Divisions moving southeast. Only the landing of 2,000 men from 284th Siberian Division saved the day. The Siberians and 13th Guards checked the advance of the German 71st Infantry Division but were not strong enough to clear the area around the landing stage and the railway station.

Farther south, the 4th Panzer Army's 14th Panzer and 29th Motorized Divisions reached the Volga and completed the isolation of 62nd Army. To their left, 24th Panzer and 94th Infantry Divisions moved through the Minina suburb, defended by the 35th Guards Division and 42nd Infantry Brigade. They were soon joined by the 92nd Naval Infantry Brigade and a ferocious fight ensued over the enormous concrete grain elevator near the banks of the Volga. This position was all that stood between the meeting of the two prongs of the 4th Panzer Army's attack and was defended by 30 naval infantry and 20 guardsmen. They drew in elements of three German divisions but eventually succumbed to overwhelming force. By 26 September, the 4th Panzer had virtually destroyed the 35th Guards Division and ground down the 92nd Naval Infantry and 42nd Infantry Brigades. The 24th Panzer Division reached the Volga and brought the landing stage under fire while the remnants of the Soviet units were evacuated across the river.

The 62nd Army had survived, but the Germans had won an important tactical victory. They controlled the Volga to the south of the city over a five-mile front. They also held the railway station and most of Mamayev Kurgan. They could bring the central landing stage under direct fire and had reduced the 62nd Army to a pocket around the industrial area in the north of the city. The Luftwaffe could keep up its interdiction efforts on the river.

There were, however, deep misgivings as the Germans had become aware that they were engaged in a completely different type of warfare. They called it *Rattenkrieg* (war of the rats). They struggled to come to terms with the effect an urban environment was having on their tactical doctrine and command system: it suffocated the application of flexible manoeuvre and the integration of airpower, tanks and infantry. The close, congested nature of the terrain, blocked as it was by ruined

buildings, rubble, cratered roads, barricades and obstacles, made rapid multi-unit manoeuvre and deployment very difficult. Blitzkrieg depended on the divisional commanders exercising flexible tactical command and initiative. If this method was to be retained in an urban environment, command decisions would have to be devolved to the battalion commanders. The battle for the city had developed into hundreds of tactical encounters at the battalion, company and platoon level but senior German officers still retained their focus on the division for planning purposes and, in their attempt to apply the command methods developed for use in manoeuvre warfare, they robbed the German forces of the very flexibility they needed. They were after victories of a scale not attainable in Stalingrad. The tempo of German attacks suffered as a result and reinforced the attritional nature of the battle. In a similar way, the heavily centralized Soviet command structure had completely failed to cope with the blitzkrieg style of warfare that the Germans had used during their summer campaigns and flexible, devolved command did not come naturally to a Soviet officer corps purged and subjugated by Stalin. The command system in Stalingrad, however, had somehow managed to adapt itself to the rigours of combat in the city. Ultimately, it was the isolation of 62nd Army that helped, as Chuikov was master in his own house and no other Soviet army

commander had the tactical freedom he had to implement his orders. He understood that close, effective and constant command and control of the battle would rarely be possible. He therefore dispensed with conventional organizational units and used what became known as the shock group, a force organized and equipped for a particular mission, consisting of between 50 and 100 men. Chuikov realized that the urban battlefield would suit small groups of heavily armed infantry that could be given orders and objectives by the divisional commander. The idea was to make the 62nd Army's pursuit of its objectives as compatible as possible with the decentralized and chaotic nature of the fighting. Soviet tanks, as opposed to their Wehrmacht counterparts, were not asked to undertake complex tactical manoeuvres but were used purely as defensive firepower, often buried in partially collapsed buildings. These tank emplacements and the Soviet artillery on the eastern bank of the Volga frustrated 6th Army's attempts to capture the city. The battle, however, was not over, as Paulus was preparing for the next round.

THE SECOND ASSAULT

The second German assault on the city came at dawn on 27 September 1942. As September progressed, so the Germans knew that winter would soon be on the way and most did not relish spending a Russian winter fighting in the ruins of Stalingrad. With little time to lose and with the fighting in the south petering out, Paulus redeployed forces to the north to strike the industrial area of the city, concentrating his attack in two thrusts. One would be against the area around Mamayev Kurgan and the Krasny Oktyabr (Red October) Steel Plant, the other striking at the Dzerzhinsky Tractor Factory where they would break through the Soviet lines, reach the Volga and turn inwards to trap the forces still to the west, who would be pinned by attacks on the Barrikady Ordnance Factory. The highly effective reconnaissance network Chuikov maintained in the city quickly detected the German redeployment and so he was able to shift some of his forces northwards to meet the threat and managed to maintain the lifeline to the eastern shore with ammunition, men and food moving westwards, while wounded, civilians and prisoners moved eastwards. The lifeline consisted of R Adm Rogachev's naval flotilla augmented by a large number of fishing boats and their crews. They fought an ongoing war of attrition with Luftflotte IV commanded by GenObst Wolfram von Richthofen which had Fliegerkorps IV (GenLt Kurt Pflugbeil), which was supporting Army Group A and Fliegerkorps VIII (GenLt Martin Fiebig), which was supporting Army Group B. By this point in the battle the majority of Luftwaffe resources were being committed over Stalingrad but these, like the ground forces committed by the German Army, were not sufficient to undertake all that was being asked of them. They managed to maintain local air superiority over the city but could not undertake both close air support for the ground troops and isolate the western bank of the Volga by interdicting the Soviet naval flotillas on the river. The Germans' inability to isolate the west bank of the Volga from the sources of men and matériel to the east with either their ground forces or their air power would prove decisive.

With an advanced warning as to the Germans' likely intentions, Chuikov moved first and attacked at 06.00 on 27 September towards

Mamayev Kurgan with the 284th Siberian and 95th Infantry Divisions, while the 13th Guards moved against the railway station. The attack was met with a fearsome response from Fliegerkorps VIII who pinned down 62nd Army for two hours after which the German 6th Army counter-attacked using a total of 11 divisions consisting of three Panzer (14th, 16th and 24th), two motorized (29th and 60th) and six infantry (71st, 79th, 94th, 100th Jäger, 295th and 389th). On Chuikov's left, the 14th Panzer and 94th Infantry Divisions consolidated their hold on the southern area of the city while 24th Panzer and 29th Motorized moved northeast. The 295th Infantry once again tried to clear Mamayev Kurgan while the 76th Infantry guarded the railway station and the 71st Infantry moved behind 13th Guards towards the Red October Steel Plant in conjunction with 100th Jäger. The 16th Panzer, 60th Motorized and 389th Infantry advanced towards the Tractor Factory from three directions. In intense fighting German forces advanced almost 3,000 yards and virtually destroyed two Soviet divisions (95th and 112th). Stavka, recognizing that a crisis point was being reached, abolished the division of responsibility for the city between the Stalingrad (Gordov) and Southeast (Yeremenko) fronts. Southeast Front was renamed Stalingrad Front and had sole responsibility for the city while, to the north, what was left of the old Stalingrad Front became the Don Front under Rokossovsky. The fighting lasted for two days and, with the arrival of fresh reinforcements (including 193rd Rifle Division), Chuikov managed to contain the German offensive, even denying them overall control of Mamayev Kurgan. Keen to maintain offensive momentum, Paulus then switched the focus of his attacks to the Orlovka salient which protruded into the German lines northwest of the city. Within the salient lay the 115th Rifle Brigade and a composite battalion, all that was left of the 112th Rifle Division. It was surrounded by German units and, on 29 September, Paulus committed 16th Panzer, 60th Motorized, 100th Jäger and 389th Infantry to enveloping it. Meanwhile, 24th Panzer continued towards the Barrikady and Red October factories and came

German infantry fighting in the outskirts of Stalingrad. Having destroyed what may have been an enemy strongpoint (in flames behind them), the soldiers have paused while the section leader gives orders about moving on to the next objective. (Nik Cornish Library)

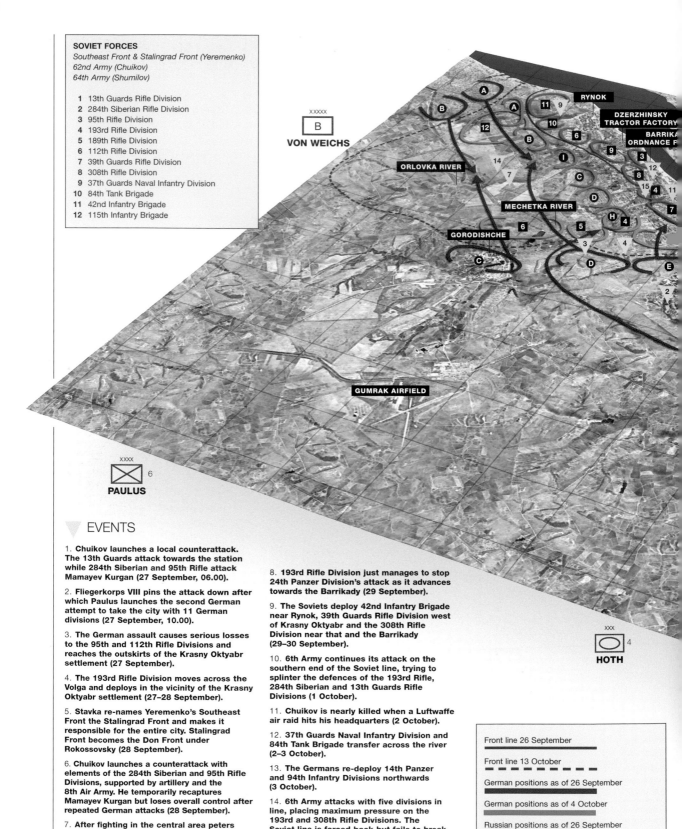

SOVIET FORCES

Southeast Front & Stalingrad Front (Yeremenko)
62nd Army (Chuikov)
64th Army (Shumilov)

1 13th Guards Rifle Division
2 284th Siberian Rifle Division
3 95th Rifle Division
4 193rd Rifle Division
5 189th Rifle Division
6 112th Rifle Division
7 39th Guards Rifle Division
8 308th Rifle Division
9 37th Guards Naval Infantry Division
10 84th Tank Brigade
11 42nd Infantry Brigade
12 115th Infantry Brigade

xxxxx
B
VON WEICHS

ORLOVKA RIVER

RYNOK

DZERZHINSKY TRACTOR FACTORY

BARRIKA ORDNANCE F

MECHETKA RIVER

GORODISHCHE

GUMRAK AIRFIELD

xxxx
6
PAULUS

xxx
4
HOTH

▼ EVENTS

1. Chuikov launches a local counterattack. The 13th Guards attack towards the station while 284th Siberian and 95th Rifle attack Mamayev Kurgan (27 September, 06.00).

2. Fliegerkorps VIII pins the attack down after which Paulus launches the second German attempt to take the city with 11 German divisions (27 September, 10.00).

3. The German assault causes serious losses to the 95th and 112th Rifle Divisions and reaches the outskirts of the Krasny Oktyabr settlement (27 September).

4. The 193rd Rifle Division moves across the Volga and deploys in the vicinity of the Krasny Oktyabr settlement (27–28 September).

5. Stavka re-names Yeremenko's Southeast Front the Stalingrad Front and makes it responsible for the entire city. Stalingrad Front becomes the Don Front under Rokossovsky (28 September).

6. Chuikov launches a counterattack with elements of the 284th Siberian and 95th Rifle Divisions, supported by artillery and the 8th Air Army. He temporarily recaptures Mamayev Kurgan but loses overall control after repeated German attacks (28 September).

7. After fighting in the central area peters out, Paulus concentrates on eliminating the Orlovka Salient with the 16th Panzer, 60th Motorised Infantry, 389th Infantry and 100th Jäger Divisions (29 September).

8. 193rd Rifle Division just manages to stop 24th Panzer Division's attack as it advances towards the Barrikady (29 September).

9. The Soviets deploy 42nd Infantry Brigade near Rynok, 39th Guards Rifle Division west of Krasny Oktyabr and the 308th Rifle Division near that and the Barrikady (29–30 September).

10. 6th Army continues its attack on the southern end of the Soviet line, trying to splinter the defences of the 193rd Rifle, 284th Siberian and 13th Guards Rifle Divisions (1 October).

11. Chuikov is nearly killed when a Luftwaffe air raid hits his headquarters (2 October).

12. 37th Guards Naval Infantry Division and 84th Tank Brigade transfer across the river (2–3 October).

13. The Germans re-deploy 14th Panzer and 94th Infantry Divisions northwards (3 October).

14. 6th Army attacks with five divisions in line, placing maximum pressure on the 193rd and 308th Rifle Divisions. The Soviet line is forced back but fails to break (4–6 October).

15. The Germans manage to capture the Silikat Factory (5 October).

Front line 26 September

Front line 13 October

German positions as of 26 September

German positions as of 4 October

Russian positions as of 26 September

Russian positions as of 4 October

GERMAN ASSAULT ON STALINGRAD: 27 SEPTEMBER–7 OCTOBER 1942

The second German assault begins on 27 September with 11 divisions. This time, constant Russian counterattacks make progress far more difficult than during the first assault and progress is difficult.

Note: Gridlines are shown at intervals of 3km/1.86miles

xxxx 62
CHUIKOV

xxxxx
Southeast Front
YEREMENKO

xxxxx
Stalingrad Front
YEREMENKO

5

KRASNAYA SLOBADA

MAMAYEV KURGAN

1 10

G

H 13

YELSHANKA

I

J

MININA

KUPOROSNOYE

K

RIVER VOLGA

xxxx 64
SHUMILOV

GERMAN FORCES
Army Group B (von Weichs)
6th Army (Paulus)
4th Panzer Army (Hoth)

A 16th Panzer Division
B 60th Motorised Infantry Division
C 389th Infantry Division
D 100th Jäger Division
E 295th Infantry Division
F 71st Infantry Division
G 76th Infantry Division
H 94th Infantry Division
I 14th Panzer Division
J 24th Panzer Division
K 29th Motorised Infantry Division

within a mile of the Volga. If it had reached the river, it could have moved into the rear of the Barrikady position and joined with the German units moving south for the assault on the Tractor Factory. It was, however, stopped by the 193rd Rifle Division.

Chuikov's men were again reinforced, by 39th Guards and 308th Rifle Divisions. For the next few days, 6th Army kept up the attack, concentrating on the 193rd Rifle Division and applying pressure to the 284th Siberian and 13th Guards in an attempt to splinter the defence. The defence held, but only just. The 6th Army, having shifted 14th Panzer and 94th Infantry north, committed 389th Infantry and 60th Motorized in an attack towards the Tractor Factory, forcing the 112th Rifle Division back. At the same time 24th Panzer forced the 308th Rifle Division to retreat back to the Silikat Factory in front of the Barrikady Ordnance Factory, while the 193rd had to retreat towards the Red October. The 6th Army now lined up to make a supreme effort with 14th Panzer, 100th Jäger, 94th and 389th Infantry Divisions attacking towards the Tractor and Barrikady factories. But as hard as the Germans pushed, they could not achieve a breakthrough, although they did force the Soviet 37th Guards, 193rd and 308th Rifle Divisions backwards, taking the Silikat Factory on 5 October. Another German attack was stalled by a Soviet artillery barrage and, after receiving orders to counter-attack, Chuikov's preparations were forstalled by an attack from the 14th Panzer Division supported by the 60th Motorized Division. They broke into the workers' settlements adjacent to the Tractor Factory but a barrage from Katyusha rocket launchers halted the attack and saved the position. The 62nd Army had been driven back but had failed to break and a desperate Paulus, after hearing that success at Stalingrad would earn him Chief of Staff at OKW (replacing Jodl), started preparing for a final offensive. He requested three infantry divisions as reinforcements but only received four specialist combat engineer battalions. Hitler was becoming more and more obsessed with capturing the city, even though Zeitzler, who had replaced Halder, had warned that the battle should be terminated. Chuikov's men had survived the second German onslaught and now the race was on to see who would finish their preparations first – the German 6th Army who were going to launch their third desperate attempt to take the city, or the Soviet 62nd Army, who were trying to rebuild their defences. The third and most critical stage of the battle was about to begin.

THE THIRD ASSAULT

As the fighting died down after the second German assault, Hitler was focusing on Stalingrad to almost the complete exclusion of the original purpose of Operation *Blau* – the seizure of the Caucasian oil reserves. On 14 October 1942, the Fuhrer issued Operational Order No. 1 stopping all German operations elsewhere on the Eastern Front except at Stalingrad and in the Caucasus. Stalingrad was now the sole determination as to whether the German 1942 summer offensive would be a success. As the 6th Army prepared itself for another offensive, it was surprised by a counter-attack from the 62nd Army. Chuikov had been ordered to improve his position by pushing the Germans back in order to increase the room available for tactical manoeuvre, something the 62nd Army would need if it was to meet the coming German attack. On 12 October, 37th Guards Division along with one regiment of the 95th Rifle Division attacked the western outskirts of the Tractor Factory. It caught the Germans by surprise and pushed them back 300 yards but the attack was forcefully stopped from going any farther as it became apparent what the Germans had amassed.

At 08.00hrs, the Germans launched their attack with three infantry divisions (100th Jäger, 94th and 389th Infantry), two Panzer divisions (14th and 24th) and the four specialist combat engineer battalions, over 90,000 men and 300 tanks concentrated on a three-mile front with massive air support. On Chuikov's far right, on the far side of the Orlovka river, was the 124th Rifle Brigade while to the south lay 112th Rifle Division with its right flank anchored on the Orlovka river. To the left of the 112th was 37th Guards Rifle Division, followed by 308th Rifle deployed in the Sculpture Park right in front of the Barrikady Factory with the 95th Rifle just behind them. South of them lay 193rd Rifle, defending the area between the Barrikady Factory and Red October Plant, 39th Guards defending the Red October, 284th Rifle directly east of Mamayev Kurgan and finally the 13th Guards. The German attack was of a scale and intensity that had not yet been seen. The central thrust

German mountain troops passing what appears to be an officer in a staff car. The Gebirgsjäger had only come into existence in 1915 and recruited mainly from the German states of Bavaria and Württemberg. The *Anschluss* with Austria provided the Wehrmacht with a large pool of trained and experienced mountain troops from the Austrian Army. (Nik Cornish Library)

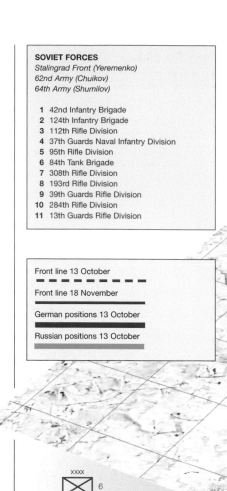

SOVIET FORCES

Stalingrad Front (Yeremenko)
62nd Army (Chuikov)
64th Army (Shumilov)

1 42nd Infantry Brigade
2 124th Infantry Brigade
3 112th Rifle Division
4 37th Guards Naval Infantry Division
5 95th Rifle Division
6 84th Tank Brigade
7 308th Rifle Division
8 193rd Rifle Division
9 39th Guards Rifle Division
10 284th Rifle Division
11 13th Guards Rifle Division

Front line 13 October

Front line 18 November

German positions 13 October

Russian positions 13 October

xxxxx
B
VON WEICHS

xxxx
PAULUS 6

RYNOK

DZERZHINSKY
TRACTOR FACTO

BARRIKAD
ORDNANCE FA

ORLOVKA RIVER

MECHETKA RIVER

GORODISHCHE

GUMRAK AIRFIELD

EVENTS

1. **Chuikov launches a counterattack with elements of the 37th Guards and 95th Rifle Divisions towards the northwest corner of the Tractor Factory, taking the 6th Army by surprise (12 October).**

2. **Hitler issues Operations Order No. 1, suspending all offensive operations on the Eastern Front, except for those around Stalingrad and in the Caucasus. Stalingrad would now become the sole determinant as to the success or failure of the summer 1942 offensive (14 October).**

3. **6th Army repulses further 62nd Army attacks and launches its third assault on the city (08.00, 14 October).**

4. **The initial attack is by three infantry divisions and two Panzer divisions, led by four specialist combat engineer battalions (14 October).**

5. **The main attack is directed against the middle of the Soviet line, in particular the 37th Guards, 112th and 308th Rifle Divisions (14 October).**

6. **14th Panzer breaks through the 37th Guards, pins the 112th Rifle (with the aid of the 60th Motorised) and reaches the Volga, splitting 62nd Army in two (14 October).**

7. **Paulus commits the fresh 305th Infantry Division to the attack on the Tractor Factory (15 October).**

8. **Chuikov receives reinforcements in the form of the 138th Siberian Division (15–17 October).**

9. **The focus of 6th Army's assault moves south with 14th Panzer, 305th Infantry and 100th Jäger Divisions advancing on the Barrikady, while 24th Panzer and 94th Infantry Divisions attack the area between the Barrikady and Krasny Oktyabr (16 October).**

10. **The 16th Panzer Division takes Rynok and continues south, putting pressure on the Soviet forces around Spartanovka in conjunction with 60th Motorised Infantry (17 October).**

11. **German forces continue to push south and overrun the 84th Tank Brigade despite stiff resistance (17 October).**

12. **Chuikov is forced to move his headquarters to behind the Krasny Oktyabr (17 October).**

13. **193rd Rifle Division finally collapses, forcing Chuikov to withdraw the 308th Rifle Division to avoid its annihilation (18 October).**

14. **The Germans secure the Tractor Factory and are fighting inside the Barrikady (20 October).**

15. **The 94th Infantry, 100th Jäger and 305th Infantry Divisions attack the remnants of the 308th and 193rd Rifle Divisions (22 October).**

16. **64th Army (Shumilov) launches diversionary attacks against the flank of 4th Panzer Army with little success (23–30 October).**

17. **Paulus launches the fresh 79th Infantry Division against Krasny Oktyabr which manages to break into the installation (23 October).**

18. **The 45th Rifle Division is moved across the river as reinforcements (26–27 October).**

19. **The 6th Army finally manages to clear the Barrikady and half of the Krasny Oktyabr (27 October).**

20. **Exhausted, 6th Army starts to scale back its operations. It holds over 90 per cent of the city and has destroyed the equivalent of seven Soviet divisions, but it is to prove not enough (29 October).**

GERMAN ASSAULT ON STALINGRAD: 14–29 OCTOBER 1942

Having lost momentum, the Germans are now subject to more powerful Soviet counterattacks such as the one launched by Chuikov on 12 October. An impasse results and Hitler becomes obsessed with victory in Stalingrad. Despite its huge gains, however, final victory for the 6th Army remains elusive.

Note: Gridlines are shown at intervals of 3km/1.86miles

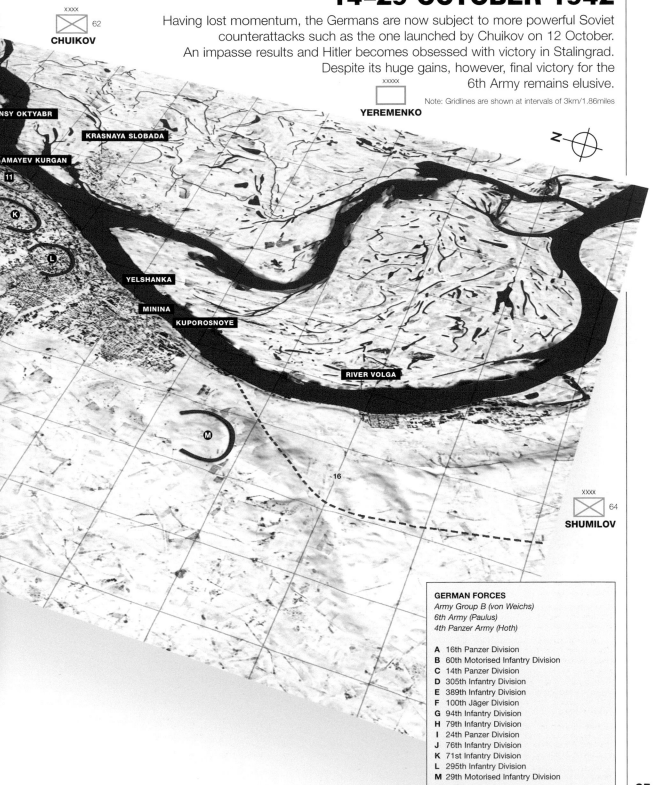

XXXX
62
CHUIKOV

XXXXX
YEREMENKO

NSY OKTYABR

KRASNAYA SLOBADA

AMAYEV KURGAN

11

K

L

YELSHANKA

MININA

KUPOROSNOYE

RIVER VOLGA

M

16

XXXX
64
SHUMILOV

GERMAN FORCES
Army Group B (von Weichs)
6th Army (Paulus)
4th Panzer Army (Hoth)

A 16th Panzer Division
B 60th Motorised Infantry Division
C 14th Panzer Division
D 305th Infantry Division
E 389th Infantry Division
F 100th Jäger Division
G 94th Infantry Division
H 79th Infantry Division
I 24th Panzer Division
J 76th Infantry Division
K 71st Infantry Division
L 295th Infantry Division
M 29th Motorised Infantry Division

was against the 112th Rifle, 37th Guards and the right flank of the 308th Rifle. The sheer weight of numbers and firepower forced open the junction between 37th Guards and 308th Rifle with most of 14th Panzer breaking through and heading northeast while 389th Infantry and 100th Jäger pinned them down. The 112th found itself enveloped by the 14th Panzer and pinned by the 60th Motorized, while the 308th was in an equally perilous position. The Germans had surrounded the Tractor factory on three sides, broken both the 37th Guards and 112th Rifle Divisions and split the 62nd Army. Chuikov decided that he could not commit additional forces to holding the Tractor Factory as it was likely that the Germans would launch an attack from a different direction after he had weakened other areas of the front. The loss of the Tractor Factory could, however, lead to the collapse of 62nd Army's right flank. The Germans then threw in the fresh 305th Infantry Division in their advance towards the factory, while 16th Panzer and 60th Motorized continued to attack southwards against Gorokhov's battered forces in the Spartanovka district. Everywhere the Soviet perimeter was forced backwards, with the Germans gaining around 2,000 yards in some places. Many Soviet units were seriously under strength and Chuikov's only reinforcement, the 138th Siberian Division would take time to deploy.

Luftwaffe ground troops with a partially camouflaged PAK 38 anti-tank gun, possibly defending one of the airfields around Stalingrad. The successor to the PAK 36, it used a larger calibre (5cm) round that was more effective against the heavier Soviet tanks, such as the KV-1 and T-34, penetrating up to 76mm of armour at 500m. (IWM, HU5168)

The Germans renewed their offensive, taking the Tractor Factory and advancing southwards with the 14th Panzer, 100th Jäger and 305th Infantry Divisions towards the Barikady, along with 24th Panzer and 94th Infantry in support to the south. However, the northern attack was halted by the dug-in tanks of the 84th Tank Brigade and Soviet artillery fire, while the 193rd Rifle and 13th Guards withstood the attacks by the 24th Panzer and 94th Infantry. Chuikov placed the 138th Siberian to the right of the 308th to defend the approach to the Barrikady. Meanwhile, the 16th Panzer and 60th Motorized Divisions had cleared much of the northern suburbs with Gorokhov reduced to a small pocket. The German forces continued their relentless pressure, advancing south towards the Barrikady and overran most of the 84th Tank Brigade in the process. This advance forced Chuikov to abandon his headquarters near the Tractor Factory and to move to a new site just behind the Red October Steel Plant. The Germans reached the edge of the Barrikady Factory and the Volga, cutting it off from the Red October. The 193rd Rifle Division was being menaced by the German 94th Infantry which was trying to break into the Barrikady. Eventually, the combined weight of the 100th Jäger, 94th and 389th Infantry forced Chuikov to withdraw what was left of the 193rd and 308th Divisions before they were annihilated. Farther south, the Germans began building up forces for an attack from the south towards the Red October while intending to pin Soviet forces in place. On 23 October, Paulus launched the fresh 79th Infantry Division against the Red October, supported by tanks and aircraft. A

company of infantry broke into the northwest corner and engaged the defenders, being quickly followed up. The Germans also overwhelmed much of the Barrikady and, although fighting would continue there for a time, it was effectively in German hands.

Two regiments of the 45th Rifle Division reinforced Chuikov on the night of 26–27 October under the command of the 193rd Rifle. The Red October was half occupied with the 39th Guards having been pushed back by the full weight of the 79th Infantry's attack – the Germans were just 365 metres from the Volga and had the landing stages under sustained fire. However, operations by the 6th Army declined after 24 October as the weather grew noticeably colder. The army was exhausted as well, worn down after two weeks of intense, gruelling combat.

The Germans held 90 per cent of the city and had the remaining pockets of Soviet territory under constant fire. They had captured the Tractor Factory and the Barrikady Ordnance Factory and had occupied half of the Red October Steel Plant. The 62nd Army had been splintered and three divisions (37th Guards, 95th and 112th Rifles) had been destroyed. Another two (193rd and 308th) were no longer fit for combat while the 84th Tank Brigade had ceased to exist as had the garrison in Spartanovka. The Germans had destroyed the equivalent of seven Soviet divisions but it was not enough. The Luftwaffe's inability to isolate 62nd Army and its supporting artillery had denied the 6th Army its ultimate triumph. This was due to the fact that Luftflotte IV just did not have the combat strength to support Army Group B's attack towards Stalingrad, Army Group A's attack into the Caucasus, interdict Soviet supplies coming into the Stalingrad region and maintain its dominance over the Red Air Force, which was gradually growing in strength. After 29 October, the fighting in the city died down except for a brief counter-attack by the fully deployed 45th Rifle Division between the Barrikady and Red October. The 6th Army could now only look forward to spending the winter amongst the ruins of a destroyed city. It was in a worse position than many imagined: the Soviets were preparing a counter-attack that would cause many in the 6th Army to die a cold death, thousands of miles from German soil.

ASSAULT ON THE RED OCTOBER STEEL PLANT,
23 OCTOBER 1942. (Pages 68–69)

In late July, Army Group B started its advance towards Stalingrad. They met fierce Soviet resistance but, by early September, the 6th Army had closed up to the Volga with 4th Panzer Army on its right flank in the southwestern outskirts of the city. Despite the initial objectives for Operation Blau, Stalingrad had gradually assumed a greater and greater psychological importance to both sides - for the Germans it became the rod that would finally break Soviet resistance and pave the way for victory on the Eastern Front. For the Soviets, the city became a symbol of their continued defiance of Nazi Germany. The assault on the city began on 14 September 1942 with von Seydlitz-Kurzbach's LI Corps attacking the centre of the city. The battle gradually developed from there with both 6th Army and 4th Panzer Army being steadily sucked into a nightmare of urban combat, trying to dislodge Chuikov's 62nd Army. The German blitzkrieg involved the coordination of armour, artillery, infantry and tanks to achieve victory, methods the Wehrmacht had used to great success. But Chuikov had discerned a weakness in that the infantry would not move before the armour and the armour rarely moved without the Luftwaffe going in first. If Chuikov could break this chain and at least lessen the impact of German airpower over the city, the Soviets might stand a fighting chance. Therefore Soviet infantry were ordered to keep as close to German positions as possible. This hampered German fighting methods and the bombing accuracy of the Luftwaffe. The huge amounts

of rubble and ruined buildings also impeded the infantry and armour from moving en masse. The battle therefore was increasingly reduced to the level of the platoon, company and battalion, rather than the division, which was still the German unit of choice but which was unsuited to this form of warfare. By mid-October, , despite these handicaps, the Germans had ground down the 62nd Army and reduced it to a small bridgehead on the west bank of the Volga. On 14 October 1942, Paulus launched his third assault on the city, the Germans being increasingly aware that winter was fast approaching. The 6th Army had concentrated three infantry divisions, two panzer divisions and four specialist combat engineer battalions on a narrow three-mile frontage with massive air support. The attack hit the 62nd Army like a sledgehammer and drove it back towards the Volga. In ten days of fighting, the Germans took the Tractor Factory and advanced south towards the Barrikady and Red October factories. On 23 October, German troops from the 79th Infantry Division (1) had reached the northwest corner of the Red October and were attempting to storm the factory against fierce opposition from Guriev's 39th Guards (2). The Germans were pressing forward with the support of armour and self-propelled guns (3), attempting to pin the Soviet defenders in place, outflank and destroy them. In this environment, hand-to-hand fighting and close-quarter assaults were the order of the day. Hand grenades and sub-machineguns, such as the MP40 (4) and PPSh-41 (5), which many German troops adopted in preference to their Kar98k bolt-action rifles (6), were the weapons of choice.

ZHUKOV SPRINGS THE TRAP

As early as 12 September in a conference with Hitler at Vinnitsa, Paulus had expressed his concern over the vulnerability of 6th Army's left flank along the Don and its right flank following the Volga. The outer flanks were guarded by formations from Germany's Axis allies (Italy, Rumania and Hungary) and, although the potential dangers of this were known to the German High Command, nothing could be done unless Army Group A was withdrawn from the Caucasus. Once again, the disparity between German ends and means was clear. The 6th Army was trapped at the edge of an enormous salient, with few reserves and fighting an intense battle of attrition, dependent on a single railway line which crossed the Don at Kalach, just 60 miles from the Soviet lines. All 21 divisions (including the 9th Flak Division) of the 6th and 4th Panzer Armies were situated in or around the Stalingrad area at the eastern tip of the salient. The three Panzer Divisions (14th, 16th and 24th) which would normally be expected to protect the flanks were in no fit state to do so. The 4th Panzer Army was a shadow of its former self, having given 6th Army all six of its remaining divisions, while 48th Panzer Corps was acting as army group reserve and that only consisted of 22nd Panzer Division and the Rumanian 1st Armoured Division, a formation equipped with Czech tanks. Hitler had promised one Panzer and two infantry divisions from France but these were not expected to arrive before the beginning of December.

To the left of 6th Army lay Dumitrescu's 3rd Rumanian Army, which had lost the Serafimovich and Kletskaya bridgeheads back in August. The Rumanians had to man a front of over 100 miles and the lack of natural barriers robbed their defences of depth. During October, Dumitrescu's proposal for a joint Rumanian–German offensive to remove the Serafimovich bridgehead was rejected as German troops could not be spared from the fighting in Stalingrad. It was a decision the Germans were about to regret. To the south of Stalingrad lay Constantinescu's 4th Rumanian Army that was just taking over command of the 6th and 7th Rumanian Corps as the Soviet counteroffensive broke. A single German formation, Generalmajor Leyser's 29th Motorized Division that had been pulled back from the city, was acting as a reserve. Thus, Army Group B was spread out over a 400-mile front with weakly defended flanks, inadequate resources, few reserves and vulnerable lines of communication. While Stalingrad had held the Wehrmacht's attention for some time, the Soviets had been looking at the wider picture.

The origins of the Soviet counteroffensive stretched back to a meeting in Moscow on 12 September 1942 between Zhukov, Vasilevsky and Stalin. In discussing what could be done, Zhukov and Vasilevsky raised the point that both the German army groups involved in the current operation were hugely over-extended and had insufficient means to complete the objectives that had been set for them (which the Soviets could reasonably guess at). The Axis supply lines were stretched thin and with satellite formations holding each flank, there might be the possibility

A German machinegun team fires at Soviet snipers hiding in some buildings nearby. It is unclear whether they are supporting another unit who is trying to flush the snipers out or are just engaging the snipers at long range. (IWM, HU5143)

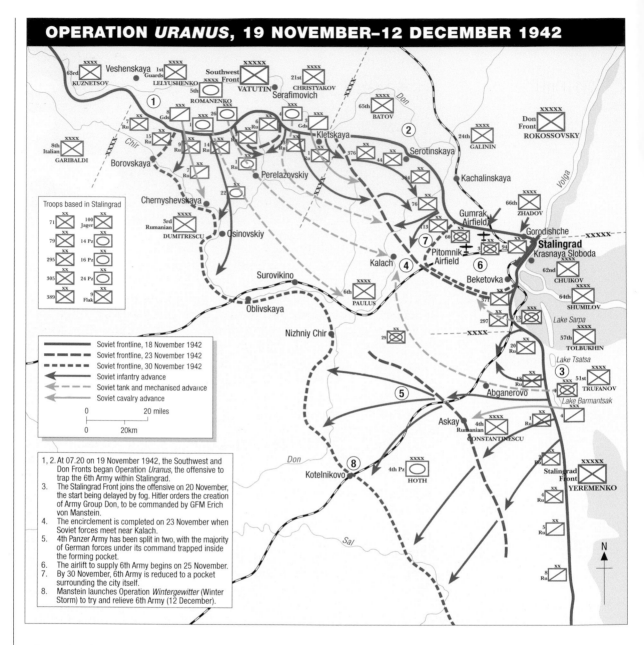

OPERATION *URANUS*, 19 NOVEMBER–12 DECEMBER 1942

Troops based in Stalingrad

71		100 Jager	
79		14 Pz	
295		16 Pz	
305		24 Pz	
389		9 Flak	

Soviet frontline, 18 November 1942
Soviet frontline, 23 November 1942
Soviet frontline, 30 November 1942
Soviet infantry advance
Soviet tank and mechanised advance
Soviet cavalry advance

0 ——— 20 miles
0 ——— 20km

1, 2. At 07.20 on 19 November 1942, the Southwest and Don Fronts began Operation *Uranus*, the offensive to trap the 6th Army within Stalingrad.

3. The Stalingrad Front joins the offensive on 20 November, the start being delayed by fog. Hitler orders the creation of Army Group Don, to be commanded by GFM Erich von Manstein.

4. The encirclement is completed on 23 November when Soviet forces meet near Kalach.

5. 4th Panzer Army has been split in two, with the majority of German forces under its command trapped inside the forming pocket.

6. The airlift to supply 6th Army begins on 25 November.

7. By 30 November, 6th Army is reduced to a pocket surrounding the city itself.

8. Manstein launches Operation *Wintergewitter* (Winter Storm) to try and relieve 6th Army (12 December).

of conducting an operation to encircle the 6th Army. It would have to be properly planned and resourced and conducted at sufficient distance away from the city so that the 6th Army would not be able to quickly disengage its armour and block the Soviet attacks. Zhukov estimated it would take around seven weeks to deploy the required forces. It would be necessary for 62nd Army to act as the 'bait' and keep 6th Army's focus on the city while preparations were made. In this way Stalingrad, despite its political and psychological significance, became a means to an end, rather than, in the German case, an end in itself. It would, however, be necessary to ensure 62nd Army's survival so Chuikov was only given enough resources to stave off collapse.

By 18 November, the preparations were complete. Yeremenko's Southeast Front had been renamed Stalingrad Front, Gordov's

Stalingrad Front had become the Don Front under Rokossovsky and a newly reconstituted Southwest Front under Vatutin came into being on the Don. The two main thrusts would be from the north against 3rd Rumanian Army moving southeast and from the east against 4th Rumanian Army moving northwest. The Southwest Front would carry the main attack in the north with 1st Guards, 5th Tank and 21st Armies. The 1st Guards was to pin the Italian 8th Army, 5th Tank was to attack in the centre, break through and exploit, while 21st Army (with help from the Don Front's 65th Army) was to attack the 3rd Rumanian Army's right flank and lever it away from the German XI Corps. Next was Don Front with 65th Army cooperating with 21st Army, while 24th and 66th Armies would pin the German forces north of Stalingrad and prevent them from interfering. The southern thrust would be from Stalingrad Front's 51st and 57th Armies which would attack and break through the Rumanian 6th Corps while 64th Army would pin the German IV Corps. The two thrusts would meet at Kalach and form a defence line.

While the Germans had had several warnings that the Soviets were preparing some sort of attack, the scale and ambition of it shocked them. This was due to the Soviet use of camouflage, concealment, disguise and deception, known as *maskirovka*. Forces were moved only at night, camouflaged during the day and kept to strict radio silence. The Red Air Force prevented sustained Luftwaffe reconnaissance and interdiction efforts and false radio nets were maintained to sustain the façade of normality. The German intelligence unit, Foreign Armies East, headed by Gen Reinhard Gehlen, was aware that Soviet forces were on the move but failed to appreciate the scale. German strategic intelligence indicated that the Soviets were not capable of undertaking more than one major counteroffensive at a time, and indications were it would be in front of Moscow, while the southern attack would either be later or a secondary operation.

This was Operation *Mars*, to be controlled by Zhukov while Operation *Uranus* would be controlled by Vasilevsky. While *Uranus* would surround the 6th Army, *Mars* would do the same to the German 9th Army in the Rzhev Salient. Operational success would be transformed into strategic victory by two follow-on offensives, codenamed Operation *Jupiter*, which would surround Army Group Centre, and Operation *Saturn*, which would be aimed at Rostov, destroying Army Group B and trapping Army

73

A slightly grainy photo of a German infantry section moving through the ruined factory district during the attack on Stalingrad. With its large buildings, many with thick walls, this area of Stalingrad became an imposing obstacle in 6th Army's attempts to take the city. (Nik Cornish Library)

Group A in the Caucasus. Gehlen's reading of the strategic situation would mean that Army Group Centre would be fully prepared for Operation *Mars* which would prove a costly failure for the Soviets.

At 07.20hrs on 19 November 1942, the Southwest and Don fronts issued the codeword 'Siren' and, ten minutes later, Soviet artillery started to pound Axis positions. Eighty minutes later, the artillery stopped and the Red Army began its attack on a 200-mile front. In the north, 1st Guards pinned down the Italian 8th Army while 5th Tank Army hit the 3rd Rumanian Army in the left flank out of the Serafimovich bridgehead while 21st Army hit their right flank out of the bridgehead near Kletskaya. The 24th and 66th Armies attacked the land bridge between the Don and Volga. Soviet forces quickly broke through the 3rd Rumanian Army but the Don Front encountered fierce resistance as Army Group B deployed the 16th Panzer Division against its 65th Army, rather than the 21st Army, whose mobile elements (4th Tank Corps and 3rd Guards Cavalry Corps) were already through the Rumanian lines. Having broken through, 5th Tank Army's mobile elements (1st and 26th Tank Corps and 8th Guards Cavalry Corps) headed southeast towards Kalach. The XXXXVIII Panzer Corps was ordered to intercept but 22nd Panzer Division lost contact with the 1st Rumanian Armoured and, instead of a powerful armoured strike force, they were committed into battle piecemeal. Army Group B ordered Paulus to halt operations in Stalingrad and deploy his Panzer divisions westwards to guard his lines of communication. With the German attention suddenly focused on the north, the southern wing of the counteroffensive struck. Yeremenko had decided to delay the attack due to poor weather but when the fog lifted his 64th, 57th and 51st Armies went into the attack. They quickly broke through the 6th and 7th Rumanian Corps who fled westwards as did 4th Panzer Army, handing a very precarious situation over to 4th Rumanian Army. The 57th Army unleashed its 13th Mechanized Corps, while 51st Army did the same with its 4th Mechanized and 4th Cavalry Corps, the two former formations heading northwest while the cavalry headed southwest towards the Aksay river. The 13th Tank Corps suffered a very painful and unexpected encounter with Leyser's 29th Motorized Division

but it was ordered to withdraw to protect the Army Group's rear. The Soviet spearheads moved on with Paulus having to evacuate his headquarters at Golubinskaya on 21 November and the bridge over the Don at Kalach falling to 26th Tank Corps the next day. The 1st Tank and 8th Guards Cavalry Corps wheeled right to secure a front line on the Chir river, 4th Tank Corps closed with the Don river, 4th Mechanized Corps continued towards Kalach and the 13th Mechanized Corps advanced northwest. Resistance was sparse and on 23 November the two pincers met just east of Kalach at Sovetsky. The Soviets believed they had trapped between 85,000 and 90,000 troops but the true figure, with 14 infantry, three panzer, three motorized and one flak divisions, two Rumanian divisions and a Croatian regiment, was over 250,000.

VON MANSTEIN'S RELIEF EFFORT

The question now facing the Fuhrer was should the 6th Army stand and fight or should it break out? With the significance, size and scale of the Soviet counteroffensive dawning on him, Hitler summoned GFM Erich von Manstein and ordered him to form Army Group Don, stabilise the position in southern Russia and prepare a relief effort. In the meantime, Hitler sought advice as to whether it would be possible to supply the 6th Army while it waited for a relief effort to be mounted. If not, there would be no choice but to organize a breakout. Hitler spoke first to GenLt Hans Jeschonnek, Chief of the Luftwaffe General Staff, who indicated that, assuming it was indeed going to be a temporary encirclement and sufficient transport aircraft and bombers were made available, it would be possible to supply the army and referred to the successful effort to supply 100,000 soldiers in the Demyansk pocket north of Moscow during the spring of 1942.

Hitler seized upon this comparison as a way of justifying his decision to forbid 6th Army to break out but 6th Army had consisted of over 250,000 men, not a mere 100,000; the time of year had been spring not winter; and the Red Air Force had been extremely weak, not gaining in strength by the day. The Demyansk Pocket had needed a daily minimum of 300 tons per day (equating to 150 aircraft per day) for which the Luftwaffe had committed 500 Ju-52s. The 6th Army calculated that they would need around 750 tons per day (or 500 tons at the barest minimum) for which it would be difficult for the Luftwaffe to find the necessary aircraft, especially with the fighting in North Africa turning against the Germans. Hitler found little real help from Göring, who, after having lost the Battle of Britain in 1940, had been out of favour with the Fuhrer and saw the airlift as an opportunity to regain favour and assured him it could be done. Zeiztler fought an unequal struggle to persuade him that an airlift was out of the question and, armed with Jeschonnek's objective study on how, even in perfect conditions, it would be nigh impossible for the Luftwaffe to supply 6th Army, confronted Göring in Hitler's presence. Hitler, however, had made up his mind and informed Paulus on 21 November that the 6th Army was to hold its positions, declaring it a *festung* (fortress) two days later. Hoth and Pickert (commander of the 9th Flak Division) as well as von Weichs, Paulus and his five corps commanders, were all of the opinion that 6th Army must attempt to break out before the Soviet lines hardened. Richthofen and Fiebig confirmed to Schmidt (6th Army Chief of Staff) that a sustained airlift during the winter was virtually impossible. Paulus was not one to disobey the Fuhrer, however, and, after flying back to Gumrak to form his new headquarters, he deployed 6th Army to undertake a rapid breakout if Hitler ordered it. The order never came and so Paulus assumed a hedgehog defence in the hope that supplies would arrive by air and a relief effort would be undertaken. They were surrounded by seven Soviet armies (62nd, 64th, 57th, 21st, 65th, 24th and 66th) guarding a perimeter of over 200 miles in length. If the 6th Army had attempted a breakout early in the siege there is little doubt the Soviets would have been hard-pressed to contain it.

Immediately after the encirclement, Vasilevsky ordered the Don and Stalingrad fronts to destroy the encircled 6th Army and plan for the next phase of operations, Operation *Saturn*, which would turn operational success into a strategic one, the ultimate objective being to take Rostov, destroy Army Group Don and trap Army Group A in the Caucasus. Thus, once *Saturn* had got underway, the relief of the 6th Army would become incompatible with overall German strategic interests (their entire force in southern Russia would be under threat) and it would have to be left to its fate. If Hitler had allowed the 6th Army to break out, Zhukov and Vasilevsky's planning would have been for nothing. However, after the initial shock of the Soviet counteroffensive, Army Group Don under Manstein was now quickly pulling itself together. The remnants of 3rd Rumanian Army and various German formations had been grouped together under GenMaj Karl Hollidt and had managed to hold the Chir river with a few bridgeheads on the eastern side. To Hollidt's right, sat Hoth's 4th Panzer Army, bereft of Panzer divisions, and far to the south of them lay 16th Motorized Division, keeping a tenuous link going between Army Group Don and Army Group A. Army Group Don was quickly reinforced with 336th Infantry, 7th and 15th Luftwaffe Field and 11th Panzer Divisions. At the end of the month Manstein also received 6th and 23rd Panzer Divisions but, while German defences were hardening along the Chir, there was little extra for forming operational reserves or a relief force, and Soviet armoured reserves were increasing

N

Legend:

Operation *Wintergewitter:*
- Frontline 12 December 1942
- Frontline 18 December 1942

Operation *Koltso:*
- Frontline 9 January 1943
- Frontline 12 January 1943
- Frontline 20 January 1943
- Frontline 23 January 1943
- Frontline 28 January 1943

Serafimovich

Kletskaya

Perelazovsky

Don Front — ROKOSSOVSKY

Kachalinskaya

Southwest Front — VATUTIN

Don

65th — BATON

24th — GALININ (4)

66th — ZHADOV

Volga

21st — CHRISTYAKOV (6)

Gumrak Airfield

6th (7) (8) **PAULUS**

Gorodische

5th — ROMANENKO

Kalach

Pitomnik Airfield

(9) Stalingrad (10)

62nd — CHUIKOV

5th Shock — POPOV

57th — TOLBUKHIN (5)

64th — SHUMILOV

Volga

Oblivskaya

Chir

(3)

Armeeabteilung Hollidt — HOLLIDT

Nizhniy Chir

Myshkova

2nd Guards — MALINOVSKY (2)

Stalingrad Front — YEREMENKO

Lake Sarpa

Lake Tsatsa

Aksay

Abgamerovo

Lake Barmantsak

Aksay

51st — TRUFANOV

17 Pz

6 Pz

Armeeabteilung Hoth — HOTH

23 Pz

Kotelnikovo

Don Front — MANSTEIN (1)

4 Rumanian — CONSTANTINESCU

0 — 20 miles

0 — 20km

1. Manstein's Army Group Don begins Operation *Wintergewitter* (Winter Storm) on 12 December.
2. The Hoth Group (17th, 6th and 23rd Panzer Divisions) reach the Myshkova River but are stopped by 2nd Guards Army's defence line, just 30 miles short (18 December).
3. The left flank of the advance was held by Armeeabteilung Hollidt, a force of approximately army size consisting of survivors from the northern Soviet pincer.
4. Meanwhile, Paulus forms a 'hedgehog' defence in 'Festung' Stalingrad.
5. Stavka give the responsibility of undertaking Operation *Koltso* to the Don Front under Rokossovsky and so all the formations surrounding Stalingrad are placed under his command on 1 January 1943.
6. *Koltso* begins on 10 January 1943 with an attack by the 21st and 65th Armies, followed by the 57th, 24th and 66th Armies. The 62nd and 64th Armies would pin German forces near the city itself.
7. Pitomnik falls on 16 January.
8. Gumrak falls on 23 January.
9. The 6th Army is split into two by the Don Front on 26 January.
10. The final pockets of German resistance surrender on 31 January and 2 February 1943.

A German armoured car. These vehicles were vital in their role as reconnaissance vehicles for the Panzer divisions, as they scouted ahead of the German advance to report back on enemy strength and dispositions. The early vehicles were designated leichter Panzerspähwagen (literally light armoured vehicle) but became better armed and armoured as the war progressed. (IWM, HU5170)

A Soviet infantry unit, moving forward in what appear to be American Willys Jeeps. The design of the Jeep was drafted by Willys-Overland in just 49 days in response to the US Military holding a competition to design a new all-terrain, robust passenger vehicle. Over 700,000 were made and the vehicle became an icon. (IWM, NY3782)

all the time. The only operation that made sense was a rapid strike northwards in conjunction with 6th Army breaking out to the south. Hitler's insistence on Army Group Don's fighting through and then maintaining a permanent link to 6th Army was one that it did not have the resources to accomplish. Von Manstein, however, endeavoured to turn Army Group Don into an effective fighting force as Vasilevsky launched the first operation to reduce the 6th Army's pocket. The attack, launched by the Stalingrad and Don fronts on 2 December, resulted in four days of fierce fighting, heavy Soviet casualties and only small gains, as the Germans were occupying the old Red Army defence positions. It was obvious that Stavka had seriously underestimated German fighting strength in the pocket and so sent additional reserves so that 6th Army could be annihilated and the perimeter held. These included 2nd Guards and 5th Guards Armies. On 9 December, the plans for Operation *Koltso* were presented to Stavka and Stalin which proposed a three-phase assault on the pocket in order to break it up prior to annihilation.

While this was being finalized, however, Manstein and Army Group Don launched their relief effort, Operation *Wintergetwitter* (*Winter Storm*) on 12 December. Von Manstein had hoped to launch a two-pronged assault with XXXXVIII Panzer Corps (11th Panzer, 336th Infantry and 7th Luftwaffe Field Divisions) advancing towards Kalach and LVII Panzer Corps (6th and 23rd Panzer and 15th Luftwaffe Field Divisions) moving northeast from Kotelnikovo, additional reinforcements had been promised, including the 17th Panzer Division, but these would not arrive before the start of the operation. However, 5th Tank Army attacked across the Chir on 30 November and, while Hollidt's forces held, it ensured that XXXXVIII Panzer Corps would have to stay there to hold the line (especially as 5th Shock Army was deploying to the area), reducing the relief effort to a single thrust by LVII Panzer Corps from around Kotelnikovo. The thrust, supported by IV

Fliegerkorps, made rapid progress against the rifle divisions of 57th Army and forced the Soviets to commit 4th Mechanized and 13th Tank Corps to blunt the offensive. The 2nd Guards Army, reinforced by 4th and 6th Mechanized Corps and 4th Cavalry Corps, was transferred to the Stalingrad Front and blocked LVII Panzer Corps at the Myshkova river. Despite von Manstein pressing Hitler to give the order 'Thunderclap' (the codeword for 6th Army to break out), no decision was made and so time was running out for both von Manstein and 6th Army.

OPERATION *LITTLE SATURN*

The Soviet High Command had proven it could react with speed in the way it dealt with Manstein's relief effort and, with this turn of events, Vasilevsky recognized that Operation *Saturn* was probably beyond the capabilities of the Red Army as the Germans had proven that they still had substantial fighting power in the area and the speed and flexibility of command to try to turn things around. Therefore a smaller-scale operation, one that would complete the isolation of the 6th Army from Army Group Don, came into being – Operation *Malvyy Saturn* (*Little Saturn*). This began on 16 December and, despite a disastrous start, after three days of bitter fighting 6th and 1st Guards Armies broke through the Italian lines while 3rd Guards advanced westwards. Their mobile units (17th, 18th, 24th and 25th Tank Corps) moved south, aiming for important targets such as the junction at Kantemirovka, the main German supply base at Millerovno, the airfields and rail junctions at Tatinskaya (today called Tatsinskiy) and Morozovsk. Southwest Front's 1st Guards Mechanized Corps was to menace Armeeabteilung Hollidt's flank and rear before moving towards Morozovsk. The 1st Guards met up with 3rd Guards on 19 December, encircling part of the Italian 8th Army, and the mobile groups were almost roaming at will, given the lack of Axis mobile reserves, with 24th Tank Corps taking Tatinskaya on 24 December.

Von Manstein reacted quickly and XXXXVIII Panzer Corps, taking advantage of a shortage of supplies on the Soviet side, counter-attacked, trapping 24th Tank Corps, which managed to escape only after being resupplied. Tatinskaya was retaken and the Germans managed to hold on to their base at Millerovno. As the tempo of Soviet operations

A photo showing a pair of Panzer III's and a Panzer II on the Russian steppe. The Panzer II was designed as a stop-gap while the designs of the Panzer III and IV were finalized. It was an enlarged version of the Panzer I, having a 2cm KwK30 L/55 cannon and increased armour, but was obsolete by 1942 and then used as a basis for a number of self-propelled artillery AFVs. (Nik Cornish Library)

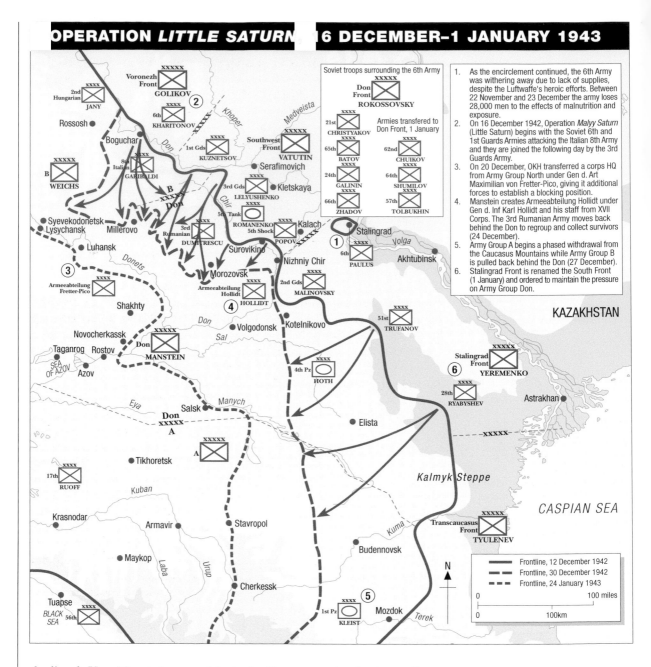

declined, Von Manstein was able to instil some order in Army Group Don's shattered left flank. While *Little Saturn* failed to gain hardly any of the specific objectives set for it, what it did do was force von Manstein to choose between the safety of Army Group Don and the strategic German situation in southern Russia and to continue to try to relieve 6th Army. With Soviet forces still advancing south and west and the dire situation facing Army Group Don, German operational and strategic interests were now best served by 6th Army remaining on the Volga and continuing to tie up seven Soviet armies. This would buy time for Manstein to reorganize Army Group Don and keep the Soviets from controlling Rostov and the retreat route for Army Group A. German forces were still over-extended, which meant there were few operational reserves with which to blunt Soviet attacks. Army Group Centre had its hands full coping with Operation *Mars* while its 2nd Panzer Army and Army Group B's 2nd Army were struggling to hold that part of the front together. On 28 December, Hitler ordered that Army Group A begin its withdrawal from the Caucasus and Army Group Don to a line 150 miles west of Stalingrad. Paulus and the 6th Army were left to their fate.

OPERATION *KOLTSO* AND THE END

With the Germans managing to retain their airbases at Tatinskaya and near Morozovsk, the airlift to 6th Army could resume. As predicted, however, the airlift had been in trouble from the very beginning with the Luftwaffe not having the available assets (in terms of types and numbers of suitable aircraft, ground assets, fighter cover and the means to deal with the harsh winter) with which to supply 6th Army even its minimum daily tonnage requirements but the operation continued through a desperate desire to relieve 6th Army's death throes and to evacuate as many wounded as possible. Hitler's indecision as to the exact purpose of *Wintergewitter* had seriously compromised the airlift as it carried bulky fuel that 6th Army would never use. Eventually, farther Soviet pressure meant that Hollidt had to retreat west in order to contain the threat posed by the Stalingrad Front and so the return to Morozovsk and Tatinskaya proved to be short lived.

After Christmas Day 1942, German morale deteriorated quickly as their fate became all too obvious. *Wintergewitter* had forced a postponement of Operation *Koltso* (*Ring*) but, with Army Group Don being forced into retreat, preparations were finalised for the total destruction of the 6th Army. The original plan was modified so the 57th Army would launch a major attack northwards, while 66th and 24th Armies attacked southwards. These would meet up with 21st and 65th Armies who would attack eastwards while 62nd and 64th Armies pinned the German forces in the immediate vicinity of the city. There would then be a general advance into Stalingrad and the elimination of the 6th Army. Stavka ordered that the Don Front should be given the responsibility of undertaking *Koltso* and so on 1 January 1943 the Stalingrad front was disbanded and the 57th, 62nd and 64th Armies transferred to the Don Front. Yeremenko would now command the South Front, consisting of 51st, 5th Shock, 2nd Guards and 28th Armies. As Stavka was finalizing the plans for Operation *Koltso*, it agreed a number of other plans to complete the destruction of German forces in southern Russia. Voronezh Front was to attack Hungarian 2nd Army, destroy it and then attack 2nd Army. This would isolate Army Group B from Army Group Don, which would be attacked on its left flank by Southwest Front and on its right by 5th Tank and 5th Shock Armies. South Front would coordinate its

A group of Soviet Naval Infantry being ferried across the Volga. With much of their fleet being bottled up in port, the USSR used the Naval Infantry as regular infantry throughout the war, although it expanded the arm greatly with ship-less sailors who had had no specific infantry training. (Nik Cornish Library)

efforts with Transcaucasus Front and aim for Rostov in order to trap Army Group A, while Transcaucasus would attack and destroy 17th Army (Operation *Gory*) and then move into the army group rear and trap the 1st and 4th Panzer Armies.

The South and Transcaucasus fronts attacked on 7 January 1943 but bad weather, difficult terrain and the poor road network hampered their advance, enabling 17th Army to withdraw towards the Kerch Peninsula and 1st and 4th Panzer Armies to retreat towards Rostov. On 12 January Voronezh Front attacked Jany's Hungarian 2nd Army. Voronezh Front broke through the Hungarian lines in several places and surrounded both it, the Italian Alpine Corps and 24th Panzer Division, although various elements fought their way out. It then turned on the 2nd Army with the support of the 13th Army from the Bryansk Front but the Germans were already pulling back and only received a battering instead of being annihilated. In a series of successive deep operations (something that had been the focus of Soviet military thought before the war) the Red Army had almost completely destroyed the German position in southern Russia.

The time had now come for the Red Army to administer the killing blow to the 6th Army. The attack was again delayed for four days in order to finish last-minute preparations and for Rokossovsky to send

A Soviet machinegun team defending a strongpoint somewhere in the ruins of Stalingrad. The weapon is an M/1910 Maxim-Sokolov, a belt-fed, water-cooled machinegun similar to the German Maxim or British Vickers and moved around by means of a small wheeled carriage. (IWM, RR1351)

surrender terms to Paulus, who rejected them. Therefore at 08.05hrs on 10 January 1943, Operation *Koltso* began, with a thunderous barrage. After two days of intense fighting, the German position in the west of the pocket began to crumble, although elsewhere the Soviets could only gain small amounts of ground against fierce German opposition. On 13 January, 21st Army became the main focus of the attack and struck out towards Pitomnik, the better of the two airfields within the pocket. The roads to the airfield were littered with the remnants of a defeated army – bodies of the dead, destroyed vehicles, wounded left to fend for themselves and men struggling to retreat in temperatures of -20°C. Many commanders selected particular officers to be flown out of the pocket at the last minute so that they could help rebuild their units in the aftermath. The airfield fell on 16 January and the last hope for 6th Army vanished. Eight German divisions (3rd, 29th and 60th Motorized, 44th, 76th, 113th, 297th and 376th Infantry) had ceased to exist as fighting formations. The Soviets continued to push towards the Volga, taking Gumrak, the last usable airfield on 23 January. By now over 100,000 German troops were congregated in Stalingrad, awaiting their fate. The Don Front moved on, crushing all in its path. Rokossovsky aimed to drive at the heart of the German defences and break them up in order to annihilate each one in turn. On 26 January, forward elements of the 21st and 65th Armies made contact with the 13th Guards Division near Mamayev Kurgan, and split the 6th Army in two. The northern pocket formed around the factories while to the south a larger pocket formed between Mamayev Kurgan and the Tsaritsa river. The reduction of the pockets continued for several days with Soviet troops fighting bitter house-to-house battles with desperate German defenders in an ironic reversal of roles. Many began to surrender, however, and, despite being raised to Generalfeldmarschall by Hitler on 31 January, Paulus surrendered to a Soviet officer that same day. Strecker refused to give in, despite most of the army now having capitulated, and Rokossovsky concentrated all of Don Front's artillery (amassing some 300 guns per kilometre) on the area to destroy XI Corps. After a withering barrage, the last German troops surrendered on 2 February 1943, after which an eerie calm descended on the city. The battle for Stalingrad was over.

SOVIET TROOPS APPROACH GUMRAK AIRFIELD, 23 JANUARY 1943. (Pages 84–85)

The gradual preoccupation of Hitler and the German High Command with the battle for Stalingrad did not stop several of those involved recognising that the 6th Army was in an increasingly vulnerable position. As early as 12 September, Paulus had raised concerns about the vulnerability of his left flank in a conference with Hitler at Vinnitsa. The flanks of the 6th Army were being held by the armies of Rumania and Italy which were not of the same quality as the Wehrmacht formations. There was also a scarcity of natural terrain which robbed the Axis defences of both depth and density. There were little in terms of reserves either as all twenty divisions of the 6th Army and 4th Panzer Army were committed to fighting for the city and Army Group B had no way of strengthening the front as long as Army Group A remained in the Caucasus and while additional reinforcements had been promised, they were not expected to arrive before December. The Germans completely underestimated the Soviets' ability to launch a major counteroffensive, despite having ample evidence of increased activity behind their lines. Operation Uranus, the codename for the Soviet attack, originated in a plan put together by Zhukov and Vasilevsky under prompting from Stalin. They believed that both Army Groups A and B were massively overextended and the result was an offensive opened on 19 November 1942, either side of the 6th Army, in an attempt to trap it in the city. The Soviets succeeded

beyond their wildest dreams and in 72 hours, the two spearheads had met near Kalach, trapping over 200,000 Germans troops. Despite this setback, the Germans started an operation to keep the 6th Army supplied by air and managed to reorganise their forces. Army Group Don, under von Manstein, attempted to break through to the 6th Army in Operation Wintergewitter. This failed, however, and with further Soviet attacks von Manstein had to withdraw his army group, leaving the 6th Army to its fate. Operation Koltso, the final push to destroy the 6th Army, was launched on 10 January 1943. Of the two airfields that had been used to keep the 6th Army supplied, Pitomnik fell on 16 January. The scene shows Soviet forces from the 65th Army (1) approaching Gumrak on 23 January, engaging German rearguards (2) who were fighting desperately to allow the last few transports to get away. As at Pitomnik, the airfield is littered with the debris of war, dead bodies and wounded left to fend for themselves. Those who were lucky enough to have been brought here by comrades have to wait in line in the cold conditions, along with officers sent there by their commanders to help reconstitute units in the aftermath, while Soviet artillery shell the airfield (3). The queues are being controlled by the German Military Police (4) who can use any and all means to maintain order, including shooting over the heads of the waiting soldiers and allowing a few men at a time onto the JU-52 (5) which might prove to be the last aircraft out of there.

THE AFTERMATH

In the early stages of Operation *Blau*, Army Group South inflicted a severe defeat upon the Red Army and drove its decimated and dispirited armies eastwards. By August 1942, the decisive victory that had eluded the Germans in 1941 seemed to be within their grasp and yet, just a few months later, the strategic situation on the Eastern Front had been transformed. Even though in the original plan for Operation *Blau*, Stalingrad had only been a secondary objective to that of the oil in the Caucasus, the issuing of Führer Directive No. 45 had meant that the objectives for the campaign had widened to the point where the two component Army Groups, A and B, would find it impossible to support each other if difficulties arose. The two objectives had become equally important and had to be achieved simultaneously rather than sequentially. It also meant that Stalingrad was to be captured, rather than merely brought under fire as a means of cutting the Volga and the supply route for the Caucasian oil. Thus the struggle for the city came to have a greater and greater psychological significance for both sides as time went on, but it was the Soviets who recognized what effect this was having on their opponents and turned it to their advantage. With the end of the battle for Stalingrad, the Wehrmacht had suffered such a serious defeat that it was obvious to all that the strategic initiative had passed to the Soviet Union. German casualties in the battle for the city itself were just under 300,000 troops (around 35,000 wounded evacuated, almost 100,000 captured and around 150,000 killed), with another 300,000 casualties suffered by the remaining German forces of Army Groups A, B and Don.

Germany's Axis allies also had high casualties, something which would have both immediate and longer term consequences. The losses incurred in *Barbarossa* had led the Germans to ask for additional Axis forces for the 1942 campaign. These forces had played a key role in manning quieter sections of the front and released German units to undertake offensive operations. The casualties suffered during the campaign meant that the Axis would be unable to support the Wehrmacht until they had rebuilt their forces. This would stretch German manpower resources to the limit. Italy suffered over 110,000 casualties which seriously undermined Mussolini's domestic position. In 1943 the Western Allies brought the North African campaign to a successful conclusion and then began preparations to invade Sicily and Italy, resulting in Mussolini's removal from power and an Italian surrender. The Rumanians suffered almost 160,000 casualties and had to rebuild their forces, while Hungary incurred some 143,000 casualties and was only able to field an army again in 1944. Just as the failure of *Barbarossa* had meant that the Germans no longer had the resources to conduct a

A pair of German soldiers outside a Russian village. The weather conditions are given away by the soldiers' clothing – greatcoats over their normal uniforms and the soldier on the right has a balaclava under his helmet. The expressions on their faces suggest they must have just been in combat and the one on the left seems to be injured. (Nik Cornish Library)

campaign with all three Army Groups in 1942, so the failure of *Blau* meant that German offensive operations had to be limited to the Kursk salient in 1943. The disparity between German means and ends, which had been apparent at the start of *Barbarossa*, was now reaching a critical point. In addition, the move by the Western Allies onto the offensive in mid-1943, first in the Mediterranean and eventually in North-West Europe, meant that the German forces in the east could not depend on reserves being transferred from the west.

A German truck driver tries to shelter his truck from the extreme cold of the icy Russian winter. The very low temperatures meant that ordinary engine oils would simply freeze solid without the use of special additives or would force the crew either to keep the engine running, something that was wasteful on fuel, or light a fire under the engine to thaw it out. (IWM, HU5180)

Immediately after the catastrophe on the Volga, the Soviets attempted to take advantage of the disruption to the German forces in the south by launching a series of offensives in southern Russia and eastern Ukraine. The overall objective was the destruction of von Manstein's Army Group South, an amalgamation of Army Groups A, B and Don. The first Soviet offensive was Operation *Gallop*, undertaken by Vatutin's Southwest Front. This was to advance west towards the lower Dnepr and the north coast of the Sea of Azov. Meanwhile, Golikov's Voronezh Front was to undertake Operation *Star* and capture Kharkov, as well as move into the Ukraine on the northern flank of the Southwest Front. There was little time for any serious preparation as the offensive was designed to follow on as quickly as possible from the success at Stalingrad. At the same time, Zhukov and Vasilevsky planned a huge operation that was to be directed against Army Group Centre, a combination of the failed operations *Mars* and *Jupiter* that had been planned to take place at the same time as operations *Uranus* and *Saturn*. Rokossovsky's Central Front (previously known as the Don Front) was to attack the German 2nd Army and 2nd Panzer Army along with the Bryansk Front and part of the Western Front. It would drive northwards from the area around Kursk towards Smolensk (the rear of Army Group Centre) and meet the remainder of the Western Front and the Kalinin Front, thereby trapping most of the army group. Unfortunately, Stavka underestimated the resilience and re-organisational skill of the Wehrmacht (and in particular von Manstein) and overestimated the capabilities of Fronts that were tired and in need of replacements (the Soviets having suffered well over a million casualties during Operation *Blau*). As the Soviet offensive got under way, von Manstein calculated that they were operating on over-extended supply lines and fostered the belief that things were going well by conceding Kharkov. At the same time, German forces that were previously in the Caucasus had withdrawn past Rostov and were concentrating in the Donbas region. On 19 February, von Manstein began his counteroffensive, led by the 2nd SS Panzer Corps, and by mid-March had severely damaged both the Southwest and Voronezh Fronts as well as forcing the Soviets to curtail the attack by Rokossovsky's Central Front, which by that time had made deep inroads into the German 2nd Army. Thus von Manstein was able to stabilize the German position, although the Wehrmacht found itself in almost the same positions it had occupied before Operation *Blau* had begun. The fighting around Kharkov was

followed by Operation *Zitadelle* in July 1943 where the Wehrmacht would
commit a significant proportion of its armoured strength in order to pinch
out the salient around Kursk in order to shorten and consolidate their line.
The Soviets had received intelligence that this was what the Germans were
planning and therefore constructed massive defensive lines in great depth
in order to absorb the momentum of the attack after which they would
counter-attack with their own armoured reserves. This they did and, after
what has been called the greatest tank battle in history, went onto the
offensive. The Wehrmacht remained a formidable force however and it
would take almost another two years before the Red Army entered Berlin.

So why did the Wehrmacht, victorious in Western Europe, fail to defeat
the Soviet Union in both operations *Barbarossa* and *Blau*, a failure that
would lead to the catastrophe at Stalingrad? It has been argued that this
failure to defeat the Soviet Union was due to the German approach to
warfare and their fighting methods. During the Second World War, the
Wehrmacht's understanding of strategy still encompassed the nineteenth-
century concept of *Vernichtungsschlacht*, which loosely translated means a

strategic military victory in a single campaign. Having the ability to destroy an enemy army through tactical and operational excellence would quickly bring about victory at the strategic level and thus attain the political objectives of the war. During the inter-war period, the German Army learnt a number of lessons from its experiences in the First World War, but refused to believe that the Schlieffen Plan, itself a powerful example of the *Vernichtungsschlacht*, had failed because of tactical flaws in its execution, but rather that the British and French armies had failed to adopt a particular tactical approach.

The success of the German blitzkrieg between September 1939 and June 1941 seemed to justify the continued use of the *Vernichtungsschlacht*. In the campaign for the Low Countries and France, both sides were evenly matched in terms of personnel, tanks and aircraft, but in six weeks, the Wehrmacht achieved what the Imperial German Army could not in four years. The Wehrmacht succeeded in these early campaigns because the opposing armies could not counter the Germans' use of manoeuvre warfare and so did not really provide a reliable test of German fighting prowess, tactics and techniques and therefore the concept of *Vernichtungsschlacht* itself. That the Germans believed it did, helps explain the failure of *Barbarossa* in 1941 and *Blau* in 1942.

In many circles, the development and employment of blitzkrieg constituted a revolutionary advance in the techniques of war, but for the Germans, who rarely used the term blitzkrieg itself, it was merely a new word used to describe already established fighting methods, albeit with new weapons. The German tactical approach to battle was again heavily influenced by the nineteenth-century concept of *Kesselschlacht* (roughly translated as a cauldron battle of annihilation) that was the practical approach to achieving a *Vernichtungsschlacht*, on the field of battle. This, in effect, involved encircling the enemy army and destroying it. In the early years of the war, the Wehrmacht used the *Kesselschlacht* concept with great success, although in fact there was nothing that was particularly sophisticated about it. It therefore followed that the number of encirclement operations would depend on the size and skill of the opponent. The Wehrmacht concentrated on achieving tactical excellence through a combination of creativity, initiative, boldness and adaptability in conjunction with a thorough understanding of the value of mechanization, airpower, artillery, communications and manoeuvre

A column of German PoWs marching off to captivity. Of the 91,000 men that surrendered, many died during their movement to the internment camps near Tashkent. Only some 15,000 were still alive by May 1943 and only 5,000 of those saw Germany again, the last in 1955. (IWM, MISC60748)

in order to encircle and destroy the enemy. However, the scale of the pockets that were created in the *Kesselschlachten* during the campaign in the east caused problems in that the Germans had essentially two armies – a mechanized force, which formed the minority and an infantry force that formed the majority. The Panzer groups would need to undertake huge encircling movements in order to trap the Soviet armies and prevent them from escaping into the interior, but would have to wait until they had been reduced by the infantry with the support of the Luftwaffe before moving on, which would eventually hinder forward momentum as the Panzer groups quickly outran the infantry. A slower advance would allow the proper elimination of the pockets but might invite an attritional struggle that would favour the Soviet Union. The widespread mechanization of the Wehrmacht was impossible at that point and so the Germans gambled on achieving a complete victory before the problem became too serious. If it worked, a campaign in 1942 (which would have to face the same problem) would be irrelevant. That the gamble came so close to success was thanks to Stalin who did not allow the Red Army to trade space for time after *Barbarossa* had begun and so gave the Germans exactly what they had been hoping for.

The Germans failed to achieve victory over the Soviet Union because of its vast manpower and industrial resources as well as its ability to force the Germans into fighting an attritional battle over a particular objective, first at Moscow and then at Stalingrad. Also, the invasion of the Soviet Union and operations on the Eastern Front involved problems that the Germans had not really confronted in the early campaigns. These revolved around geography, distance, time and scale and their effects were increasingly felt during the campaigns of 1941 and 1942. Geographically, the Pripet Marshes dominated the western part of the Soviet Union so that operations in the south were isolated until the Wehrmacht had advanced into the Ukraine. The size of the Soviet Union and the distances involved also affected German operations and logistics. The Panzer force had suffered wear and tear during the battle for France but, as it was only some 200 miles from the Ardennes to the Atlantic coast, supporting the campaign was relatively easy. The distance from Warsaw to Moscow, however, is around 1,000 miles; from Leningrad to Rostov around 1,200 miles; and from Berlin to Stalingrad around 2,000 miles. Therefore supplies of food, ammunition and spare parts, fresh equipment and replacement personnel had to move much greater distances than before. The Russian climate limited mobile operations to between the months of May and November, so the time of year became important. All this, and the scale of operations that the Wehrmacht had to undertake, was greater than anything previously attempted in a country where the lack of a modern infrastructure hindered the logistic support of rapid mobile operations even under the most favourable of conditions.

The cost of defeat. A moving picture showing a dead German soldier lying where he fell as daylight draws to a close and the sun begins to set. The loss of over 250,000 men was a staggering blow to the Wehrmacht and ended Germany's chances of decisively winning the war in the East. (Central Museum of the Armed Forces, Moscow)

THE BATTLEFIELD TODAY

Stalingrad was originally founded in 1589 as the fortress of Tsaritsyn at the confluence of the Volga and Tsaritsa rivers in order to protect the unstable southern borders of the Russian Empire. It saw heavy fighting during the Russian Civil War when it was defended by Bolshevik forces under Joseph Stalin, Kliment Voroshilov and Semyon Budenny in 1918 but captured by White Forces under Anton Denikin. After the Civil War it was renamed Stalingrad (literally Stalin's City) in 1925, in line with the Soviet practice of renaming towns and cities after notable personalities related to the revolution. The city became a centre for heavy industry during Stalin's regime but was virtually destroyed by the Second World War battle. Reconstruction began shortly after the end of the battle and the city was awarded 'Hero' status in 1945. King George VI presented the city and its citizens with a jewelled sword in recognition of the bravery they had shown. In the decades after the battle, a number of foreign cities established 'friendship' links with Stalingrad, including a number that had suffered during either the Second World War or in post-war conflicts. These include Coventry (1943), Ostrava (1948), Hiroshima (1972), Cologne (1988) and Chemnitz (1988). It was during the Cold War period in 1961 under Nikita Khrushchev's programme of destalinization that the city was renamed once again as Volgograd. This was, and still remains a contentious issue, given the international fame and recognition accorded the name Stalingrad and there have been proposals through the years for a reversion to the name but none have been accepted by either the Soviet or Russian governments.

Today, Volgograd is still an important industrial city. Its industries include oil refining, shipbuilding, the manufacture of vehicles and industrial machinery, aluminium and steel production and chemicals. In addition, a large hydroelectric plant operates just north of the city. It is a major railway junction, linking Moscow with the Donbas region of the Ukraine, the Caucasus and Siberia. It stands at the east end of the Volga–Don Canal that opened in 1952 to link the two rivers and astride European Route E40, the longest road link in Europe that connects Calais with Ridder in Kazakhstan. As far as memorials to and remnants of the battle are concerned, there are stark ruins preserved near the Afghan War Memorial, a reminder of the disastrous conflict that proved to be the Soviet Union's last war, fought between December 1979 and February 1989. The main memorial, however, is at Mamayev Kurgan, which is a low hill located just outside the city centre and is topped by an 85-metre high allegorical statue of Mother Russia. In Russian, the name means the 'tumulus of Mamai' suggesting the burial place of the leader of the Tartar Golden Horde in the 1370s, although there is no historical evidence to indicate that this is indeed the case. The hill saw ferocious fighting between the German 6th Army and elements of the Soviet 62nd Army as it is the dominant height over the city, appearing on military maps as 'Height 102'. After the battle ended, the ground was ploughed up and was thought to contain between 500 and 1,250 pieces of shrapnel per square metre. The soil remained black during the battle and remained so for several springs afterwards as grass was slow to grow back and the sides of the hill had become flattened due to the intense artillery bombardments. After the war, the Soviets planned and constructed a gigantic memorial complex on the hill, which was built between 1959 and 1967, designed by Yevgenny Vuchetich. The main statue is called 'The Motherland Calls!' (*Rodina Mat' Zovyot!*) and at the time was the largest free-standing statue in the world, held on its plinth purely by its own weight. The entire structure is made of concrete except the sword's blade, which is stainless steel.

Elsewhere, as one enters the memorial complex, there is a 17-metre-long, eight-metre-high multi-figured memorial depicting a remembrance procession of people with half-lifted banners, wreaths and flowers. This is followed by the Entrance Square and a stone stairway that leads to a boulevard that is lined by poplar trees. This leads into a memorial square to 'Those who fought to the death' that contains a circular pool, within which is a statue of a soldier grasping a PPSh-41. Immediately after this is another set of stairs that narrows gradually and passes two sets of statues that were designed to look like walls that had been in the battle but which depict scenes from the fighting. Past these is another memorial square, the 'Square of the Heroes' that contains a rectangular pool, another wall that is shaped like an unfurled banner and six double-figured statues, each depicting a scene of bravery. At the back of this area are stairs and a wall, about 120 metres long with carvings of soldiers and at the foot of which is buried a time capsule with messages from soldiers and civilians who fought in the battle, which is to be opened in 2045, the 100th anniversary of the defeat of Nazi Germany. At the foot of these stairs is the entrance to a memorial hall that contains the names (engraved on red basaltic 'banners') of 7,200 defenders of the city. At the top of the stairs, there is the 'Square of Sorrow' in which Marshal Vasily Chuikov, commander of the 62nd Army which defended the city, is buried, the first marshal to be buried outside Moscow. After the 'Square of Sorrow' comes a short climb to the central monument as well as a relatively new Military Memorial Cemetery that was created in May 1994.

BIBLIOGRAPHY

Akins, W. *The Ghosts of Stalingrad*, Research Paper, Army Command and General Staff College, Fort Leavenworth, KS 66027-1352 (June 2004)

'Battle for Stalingrad' Resources Index on *About.com* website, located at http://history1900s.about.com/cs/stalingrad/index.htm (as of 16 October 2005)

'Battle for Stalingrad' Supplement to *Soviet Military Review*, Number 12 (1982), Krasnaya Zvezda

Beevor, A. Stalingrad, Penguin, London (1999)

Carell, P. *Stalingrad – The Defeat of the German 6th Army*, Schiffer Publishing, Atglen, PA (1993)

Fowler, W. *Stalingrad – The Vital 7 Days*, Spellmount, Staplehurst (2005)

Glantz, D. *From the Don to the Dnepr*: Soviet Offensive Operations, December 1942 – August 1943, Frank Cass, London (1991 [Reprinted 2002])

Jukes, G. *Stalingrad: The Turning Point*, MacDonald & Co, London, (1968)

McTaggart, P. 'Winter Tempest' in *World War II* magazine, November 1997, located online at http://history1900s.about.com/library/prm/bltempestinstalingrad1.htm (as of 16 October 2005)

Overy, R. *Russia's War*, Penguin, London (1999)

Rotundo, L. *Battle for Stalingrad* – The 1943 Soviet General Staff Study, Pergamon-Brassey's, London (1989)

Showalter, D. 'Stalingrad' in *World War II* magazine, January 2003, pp. 30 – 38, 88

Smith, D. *Commonalities in Russian Military Operations in Urban Environments*, Research Paper, Army Command and General Staff College, Fort Leavenworth, KS 66027-1352 (June 2003)

Spartacus Educational Website. Located at http://www.spartacus.schoolnet.co.uk/ (as of 01 November 2005)

Thyssen, M. *A Desperate Struggle to Save a Condemned Army – A Critical Review of the Stalingrad Airlift*, Research Paper, Air Command and Staff College, Maxwell AFB, AL 36112 (March 1997)

Walsh, S. *Stalingrad 1942 – 1943 The Infernal Cauldron*, Simon & Schuster, London (2000)

Wieder, J and von Einsiedel, H. *Stalingrad: Memories and Reassessments*, Cassell Military, London (2002)

Yoder, M. 'Battle of Stalingrad' Webpages, part of the *Military History Online* Website, located at http://www.militaryhistoryonline.com/wwii/stalingrad/default.aspx (as of 20 March 2006)

Ziemke, E and Bauer, M. *Moscow to Stalingrad: Decision in the East*, Military Heritage Press, New York (1988)

INDEX

References to illustrations are shown in **bold**.